# STILL IN THE GAME

## FINDING THE **FAITH** TO TACKLE LIFE'S BIGGEST CHALLENGES

## DEVON STILL

WITH MARK DAGOSTINO

W Publishing Group

An Imprint of Thomas Nelson

Published in Nashville, Tennessee, by W Publishing, an imprint of Thomas Nelson.

Thomas Nelson titles may be purchased in bulk for educational, business, fund-raising, or sales promotional use. For information, please e-mail SpecialMarkets@ThomasNelson.com.

Unless otherwise noted, Scripture quotations are taken from the Holy Bible, New International Version®, NIV®. Copyright © 1973, 1978, 1984, 2011 by Biblica, Inc.® Used by permission of Zondervan. All rights reserved worldwide. www.zondervan.com. The "NIV" and "New International Version" are trademarks registered in the United States Patent and Trademark Office by Biblica, Inc.®

Scripture quotations marked NET are from the NET Bible®. Copyright © 1996–2006 by Biblical Studies Press, L.L.C. http://netbible.com. All rights reserved.

Any Internet addresses, phone numbers, or company or product information printed in this book are offered as a resource and are not intended in any way to be or to imply an endorsement by Thomas Nelson, nor does Thomas Nelson vouch for the existence, content, or services of these sites, phone numbers, companies, or products beyond the life of this book.

ISBN 978-0-7852-2246-0 (eBook)

Library of Congress Control Number: 2018909535

ISBN 978-0-7852-2242-2

Printed in the United States of America
18 19 20 21 22  LSC  10 9 8 7 6 5 4 3 2 1

# CONTENTS

# PREFACE

>> Life has a way of bringing you to your knees. At some point or another, no matter how strong you are, no matter how in control you think you are, you will drop to the ground and pray. And pray hard.

In my case, I was less than two years into what I thought were all of my dreams coming true. I had made it to the NFL. I was a defensive tackle for the Cincinnati Bengals. I was making good money. I had a girlfriend I loved, who loved me back. And I like to think I cherished all of those blessings just a little bit more than some of the young guys around me because I had a daughter to share it all with me.

My daughter. My Leah. The beautiful little girl with the big bright smile who came into my life before my senior year of college, who inspired me to get busy not just dreaming of a better life but achieving it.

On June 2, 2014, my then four-year-old daughter was diagnosed with cancer.

When I heard that word, I fell to the ground, and I honestly didn't know where I would find the strength to stand back up. I didn't know how I would ever be able to be strong enough to help my little girl face this disease. I was devastated, scared, in shock, and overwhelmed. How could this happen to my Leah? My little angel. How would I ever find the strength to battle this?

I didn't know then what I know now.

In truth, I didn't know God's power, and I didn't recognize the power that God had given to me.

What I didn't know then was that God had already been working, preparing me with every obstacle I had ever overcome, to face every obstacle that now lay in front of me.

I didn't realize He had been there every step of the way.

I didn't realize He was with me, even then, right there in that hospital, in a moment when I felt more abandoned by God than I'd ever felt in my life.

I didn't realize that through Leah, God was about to reveal He'd already blessed me with a Playbook for Life. A playbook I would finally recognize. A playbook I recognize now when I look back on the important moments of my life, and which I have the good fortune to share with others all over the world through the internet, through speaking engagements, on TV, and right here in the pages of this book. I had no idea He would use this challenge to set me and my daughter on a path of purpose that was much bigger than either of us ever could have imagined.

I didn't realize then that God works that way in all of our lives. Every day. And it's up to each of us to get off the bench, to stand up, and to get in the game no matter what life throws at us, so we can feel the full power of His blessing.

I realize all of that now. I'm thankful for it. And that's why I'm writing this book.

Whether you're a believer or not, whether you're a churchgoer or not, whether you picked up this book in the hopes of finding some divine inspiration or just picked it up looking for a little advice to help get you where you want to go in life, I hope that by the end of this book you'll see it too. In your own way, in your own life, God has been leading you down the path to where you are now; and even at this very moment, He is giving you the tools you need to handle whatever life throws at you next.

You just have to do your part in order to realize those blessings.

What I know now, what I'm finally able to see, is that God had been giving me what I needed—and therefore giving me what my daughter would need—going all the way back to the very beginning of my life.

# CHAPTER ONE

# PREGAME

>> Playing basketball with my dad is the most prominent memory I have of my early years, right up until the third grade.

My parents, along with me, my older brother, Tony, and our baby sister, Shaquara, all lived in a white brick, two-story duplex in a place called Cambridge—an affordable housing community on the outskirts of Wilmington, Delaware. That spot up on a hill overlooking the Delaware River was a pretty good place for a kid like me to grow up in the early 1990s. We lived on Kynlyn Drive, and there were patches of grass in between all the brick buildings with plenty of space to get outside and play. There were lots of kids in the neighborhood looking to play every day. It was fun.

When it came to basketball, though, my dad never went easy on us. Not even once. We'd walk up the alleyway to the court when I was six, seven, eight years old, and my big brother and I would take turns squaring off one-on-one against our father. He's six feet, two inches tall. We were little kids. Yet he'd whoop us every time. No mercy.

"C'mon now, Devon, take the shot. Take the shot!" he'd say.

I'd take one more dribble, go to plant my feet, and he'd shoulder in, steal the ball, turn around, and toss up a perfect jump shot. *Swoosh.* The man was good at the game, and it was right there on that raggedy old concrete basketball court with my dad where I first fell in love with the sport. With any sport, for that matter.

Basketball was my father's passion, and he wanted us to be passionate too.

"You're not gonna get any better if I go easy on you now, are you?" he'd ask with a big smile on his face.

"Someday I'll beat you," I'd holler back at him, in the most serious voice I could make. "You just wait. I'm gonna be big as you and tall as you and you're goin' *down*!"

"That's what I'm talkin' about!" my dad would say, laughing as he tossed the ball out to me, then stole it again before going in for the game-winning layup. "Alright, we'd better get inside before dinner's on the table, or you know your mom will be mad."

Tony and I were lucky enough to have bikes as kids, too, and when the weather was good, those bikes were just about all we needed to entertain ourselves all day long. We used to see BMX riders on TV, and we'd pretend to be just like them on those patches of grass between the sidewalks. We'd get busy building ramps and jumps out of old milk crates and pieces of wood we'd find piled against the fences behind the buildings. I still remember the rush of getting up on a little embankment, perching that bike on the edge, then pedaling hard as I could 'til I hit that ramp and flew through the air. I imagined I was taking some great big leap, when in reality I was probably only clearing a foot or so before landing back down on the pavement. It sure felt amazing to catch some air, though.

We didn't wear helmets, of course. Nobody did. Sometimes it's a wonder we're still alive. I remember one time Tony didn't pedal fast enough and instead of flying up into the air when he hit the top of the ramp, his front wheel fell straight down. The back of the bike flipped up, and he nosedived into the ground. He started crying and my mom came running out of the house yelling, "I told you this was gonna happen!" even as she hugged him, wiped the dirt from his face, and took him inside to put a Band-Aid on his chin.

My mom was always cleaning up after my brother and me. Whether we were making a mess of our knees and elbows (and chins) or tearing up the apartment, she was always there to put everything back in place. She liked to keep a neat house. I don't think she'd be bothered if I said she was obsessive about it. She was so proud of how nice she kept the place, she didn't even bother giving my dad or us boys a list of chores to do, mainly because she knew we wouldn't clean things up as good as she wanted. She was much happier if we stayed out on the basketball court and out of the way while she cleaned and cooked.

Mom would be cleaning around my dad while he watched football on Sundays too. He was almost as passionate about watching football on Sundays as he was about playing basketball. It drove us nuts sometimes, the way that TV would stay on all day with game after game. It felt like we couldn't drag him away from the TV no matter what we did. In fact, I resented the fact that football existed because it took so much of my dad's attention on all those Sundays when we could have been out playing basketball.

I suppose if that's all I had to complain about as a kid, I was living a pretty good life.

• • •

My mom and dad are my heroes, but if you asked my mom, she would say: "We didn't do nothing special. We did everything like every other parent out there is doing, raising their kids, teaching them right, doing what they are supposed to do."

My mom, Melissa, who most people call Missy, was raised with a strong family background. Her grandparents were a big part of her life and helped to raise her all the way up to high school. That may sound funny to think about, having your grandparents there every day, but it wasn't uncommon in those days. There were a lot of young mothers in the '60s and '70s, and families would stay close out of choice but also necessity. Her grandparents took her and her sisters to church every Sunday, and "living right" and "doing right" were a big part of daily life.

When her own mother's marriage ended unexpectedly in divorce, my mom was only seven. It was just assumed that everyone had to pitch in to help while her mom worked from six in the morning until seven at night after that, which meant my mom's job from that moment on was to take care of her two younger sisters. It was the "right" thing to do—but the cost was her education. My mom didn't complain, though. Everyone in her family knew hard work, and they did it with grace. Mom could have been bitter or angry at her own dad or at her own mom, but she wasn't. She watched her mom work long, hard hours to make sure that they had a house and food to eat, and she was grateful.

"Families work together," she always told me. "They do what's needed for each other."

After a few years of taking care of her sisters and then working to help out, though, she realized what her dedication had cost her. She decided that no matter what, if she ever had children, she would see to it that they got a good education.

My dad, Antonio, was also raised by a single mom. His mom loved him very much, but he barely knew his own father. "He just wasn't around," he told us. He had seen him a few times. His father took him to see a Bruce Lee movie once or twice. But when his father died during his senior year of high school, two days after my dad's birthday, my dad didn't even know how to feel. It was at that moment he decided that if something ever happened to him, he didn't want his own children to feel that way. He decided to do the opposite of what his father had done. He made a decision to always be there for his kids. He would know them and support them and help them succeed in life.

My mom and dad met in high school, when she was in tenth grade and he was a senior, but they didn't start dating until after he'd gone off to Benedict College for half a semester. He came back to town after his dream of making it as a basketball player didn't pan out the way he'd hoped, and that summer they happened to run into each other on the way to the local Pathmark grocery store. They started hanging out a lot after that, and by the time my dad was twenty-one, they were starting a family.

Given their backgrounds, I guess it's no wonder both of my parents wanted their kids to be disciplined. They insisted that we do the "right thing" and "live right." My mom's mom even dragged us off to church most Sundays, just like my mom's grandmother had done every Sunday of her life. We resisted at the time, but I suppose the lessons we learned on those Sundays became the seeds of faith that would grow later in life.

My brother, Tony, and I were actually born up in Camden, New Jersey—which, if you don't know Camden, I think it's safe to say it was a really rough town. For years it was ranked as the deadliest city in America. The only reason I didn't grow up in that violent environment is because when I was two years old, our house in Camden burned down. No one got hurt, but my parents lost everything. My brother and I don't have any baby pictures because they all got burned up in that fire. And yet, that fire was the reason we moved someplace a little safer.

My mom heard there were lots of job opportunities down in Delaware, and the city of Wilmington had affordable housing in what seemed like some pretty nice neighborhoods. So that's where we up and went.

Wilmington was a rough town too. It just wasn't quite as rough as Camden, or at least it wasn't back then. In the 1980s, Wilmington had become a major banking hub. Look on your credit card statements. Chances are that's where you're sending your monthly payments. But the profits from those big banks didn't spread out into the community. In fact, by the early '90s more and more neighborhoods in Wilmington fell victim to drugs and violence, not unlike what happened in a lot of big cities during and after the so-called "boom times." Even so, for my parents, Wilmington seemed like a big step up. A place to rebuild. A place to start fresh.

For me? It was the only life I knew. I don't remember life in Camden. I remember life on Kynlyn Drive, with a dad who loved playing basketball with me and my brother, and a mom who showed her love in every corner of our neat and comfortable little home. We were too young to know what was going on after dark. I was too young to fully comprehend just how rough this city was just a few blocks south of where we rode our bikes every day. My parents did their best to shelter us from all of that for as long as they could. They sheltered us from a lot of things.

I loved my life. I loved my parents. I loved my brother and my baby sister, Shaquara, who was born six years after me. I loved having so many friends around all the time. In fact, if things had stayed just like that for the rest of my life, I think I would have been perfectly happy.

But sometimes the things you don't see can sneak up on you.

•  •  •

One night, right in the middle of my third-grade year, my parents got into a huge fight. Tony and I stayed behind our bedroom door while the fight played out, but that apartment was small, and we couldn't help but overhear them. My mom kept yelling something about him always being out too late. Then my dad was yelling something about something my mom did. At one point my dad took his watch and threw it out the door. My brother and I both thought his watch was cool, so we ran out into the grass and looked for it but never found it. Inside, the fighting continued. Something about money. Something about where my dad was always going off to. And then sometime late that night, my mom grabbed my baby sister and left. She just left.

In the morning my dad said, "I don't know, boys. I don't think she's coming back. I think your mom and I are getting a divorce."

I lay on the couch in our living room and cried all that day, just wishing and praying for my mom to come back. But with every passing hour it became clear that she wasn't going to.

I had always thought my parents got along. I was sure they loved each other. I didn't understand what was happening. It wouldn't be 'til I was a whole lot older that I'd have any idea about the grown-up problems they had—the money issues, my dad's gambling, my mom's suspicions and retaliations, the relationship problems that had quietly torn them apart while my brother and sister and I were busy playing or sleeping.

I know now that both of my parents had strong commitments to what they wanted to do and be for their own children, but unfortunately they had few examples of how a wife and husband make it work over the long term. Times being what they were and lacking in higher education, they lived day to day and they struggled to provide for us. We didn't know that then. We always had lights and food. It might not have been the food we wanted, but there was always something in the house. Part of mom's idea of living right was making sure us kids wouldn't see the things that they were dealing with as grown-ups. They both tried hard to keep normalcy in the household, so we had no idea how hard things were for them.

So to me, to us kids, it all came out of nowhere.

One night, one argument, and our whole world changed.

A few days later, I overheard my dad on the phone talking about a tax refund and something about losing the apartment. My dad seemed real worried that we were going to wind up on the street, and he wasn't about to let that happen to his kids. So he tracked down where my mom had moved to—just a few miles away in the suburb of Claymont—and he asked us to pack a few things and he drove us up there in his big old white Buick. He drove around just looking for some sign of her, and when he spotted a kid on a bike delivering newspapers, he pulled over and asked the kid, "Did anybody new just move into this neighborhood?"

"Yeah," the kid said.

"Can you show me where?" my dad asked, and we followed the kid on the bike down the street until he pointed. My dad pulled over in front of a row of apartments that I had never seen before and he got out of the car. He told us to come with him, and we walked up to the door. He knocked and then he told us to stay there as he walked slowly back toward the car. A few seconds later, my mom opened the door.

"Mom!" we both shouted, and she wrapped her arms around us and gave us a big hug. My dad got back in the car and drove away without a word. That was that. From that point forward, my mom said, we would live with her.

We never went back to Kynlyn Drive. Our toys and clothes and things showed up in the next day or so. My dad must have packed everything up and brought it over in the middle of the night or something, because we didn't see him and we weren't sure when we were going to see him again.

I didn't know how to make sense of it all.

Once again, my whole world changed. Just like that, I found myself living in an apartment complex in the suburbs, with my mom taking me down in the morning to enroll me in a brand-new school: a one-story elementary school set off the main road, hidden by a bunch of trees and filled with a whole lot of kids I didn't know. I felt like an outsider on day one, and I could tell by the way some of the other boys were looking at me that there was going to be trouble. I wasn't tall yet, and I certainly wasn't intimidating, but I was bigger than most kids my age. That made me a pretty good target. Sure enough, at the end of the day, a group of about ten of them gathered together in front of the school and kept looking over at me until all I could think was, *Run!*

Those boys started chasing me, and I was scared. I barely remembered the way to get back to our new apartment, but even at that age I was fast. Faster than the length of my legs or the size of my body would let on. Thankfully, I easily outran those boys and made it home.

It turns out they weren't going to hurt me. Chasing me down was more of an initiation or something. I would wind up becoming friends with most of them over the course of the second half of that school year. But on that day, I was scared. And I ran into our new apartment all out of breath to find no one home to rescue me.

In order to support us in her new role as a single mom, my mother took two jobs. The first was as an executive assistant at one of the big banks in Wilmington, and the second was in the evening as a cashier at Kmart. Those afternoons and evenings without a parent home left my brother and me fending for ourselves. We were forced to grow up real fast. And with a whole lot of unsupervised time on our hands, we found trouble.

I was angry about the whole situation, and I let my mom know it. I had never talked back to my mom before, and the first time I did, she yelled at me. She let me know I was wrong. But I wasn't scared of her. I knew she wouldn't lay a hand on me. If I left a toy on the table or something, she might yell and throw it at me, but I knew her raised voice would be the end of it. So I didn't back down.

The next time I talked back to her, she called my dad.

In fact, I'm pretty sure the first time I saw my dad after the split was when he came to discipline me for talking back to my mom. I was surprised that he came to her defense, and I didn't even care if he beat me for mouthing off to her. I was just glad to see him.

Like most kids, I just wanted both of my parents in my life. And I learned that day that the quickest way to get to see my dad was to get into trouble. So I kept on getting in trouble and kept talking back to my mom, just so I'd get to see him.

My dad, being the disciplinarian he was, decided that I just had too much time on my hands. So that fall, when I moved on to yet another school—Claymont Elementary, for fourth grade—he enrolled me in the football program. He kept talking about structure and teamwork and dedication to the game, the same way he talked on the basketball court. I didn't take it seriously at first. I had played football with friends and thought it might be fun, so I went along with it. But then, at our very first practice, out on a playing field that was only separated from a great big highway by a thin row of trees, I discovered just how tough organized football could be.

I went out there all proud to be wearing a purple-and-white shirt to play for the Claymont Falcons, thinking this was going to be easy. And then out at midfield at that very first practice, I got hit. Hard. One of my teammates slammed into my stomach, helmet first. Knocked the wind right out of me, and I fell to the ground. I could not believe how much it hurt. But nobody was even making a fuss about it. "Come on, man. Get up!" they all said, as if this pain I was feeling was a totally normal part of the game.

That one hit was enough to make me want to quit. Why would anyone want to play football? But my dad, the disciplinarian, wasn't having it.

"There is no way a son of mine is going to give up after one practice and one bad hit!" he said to me. "You're going back tomorrow, you're going to take it like a man, and the next time you have a chance to hit that kid, make sure he feels it. When you play your first game, I'm gonna be there to watch you, alright? You're gonna make me proud, Devon."

I liked the thought of that—not just of making him proud, but of having him there in the stands to watch me. I'd think of that every time I wanted to quit.

There was just one problem: I wasn't allowed to play. I was too heavy. I outweighed the other kids in the league by so much, the officials decided it was a safety hazard to put me on the field. I was embarrassed by my weight. We had to weigh ourselves in gym class one time and write our weights up on the board, and while all of the other kids were coming in at fifty, sixty, maybe seventy pounds, I was over one hundred. It bothered me so much that I lied about it. I went to the board and wrote down some number significantly lower than a hundred just so no one would make fun of me. But in football, I couldn't lie. The coach had no choice but to keep me on the bench.

Whether it was because of that or for some other reason, I started getting into trouble again. My grades dropped too. So my dad pulled me from the team entirely. He said I couldn't play any other sports the whole rest of that year unless I stayed out of trouble and got my grades up.

That didn't happen. I didn't want to do the right thing. I was stubborn. And the kind of trouble I was getting into was about to get worse.

# CHAPTER TWO

# COIN TOSS

>> In fifth grade, in addition to talking back to my mom, I started talking back to my teachers. I talked back to a lot of other kids, too, and started getting into fights with some of those kids in the bathroom. I did it so often that I wound up landing in-school suspension all the time—and yet every single time was worth it to me because my dad would show up.

After a few months, though, I started getting into trouble in ways that weren't about getting to see my dad. I started doing things that I knew were wrong just because that's what I thought I needed to do to survive and to get things I wanted. My parents always said they were low on cash, which meant they couldn't give it to me, which meant I had to figure out a way to get some without having to ask them for it.

Since there didn't seem to be any jobs for a kid my age, the easiest answer was stealing.

The first time I walked into a store and walked out with a candy bar without getting caught, it felt good. It tasted good too. So, it didn't take long before I started stealing all sorts of stuff from the stores in our neighborhood. I just walked in and walked right out with whatever I wanted and never got caught. There were still times when I needed cash, though, and I figured the best way to do that would be to steal it too. I even figured out ways to grab some money during the school day. For example, when teachers collected money for field trips and put it all into one of those manila envelopes, the envelope would wind up in the guidance counselor's office. The counselor's office was right across from the boys' bathroom in our school, so I would wait for her to leave, run in, grab the envelope, run into the bathroom and take all the money out, then run back and put the empty envelope back on her desk. If you get away with that sort of thing often enough, you start to think it's normal. You start to think you're above the law. You think the rules don't apply to you. And that's exactly where I was headed.

Having cash felt powerful. It meant I could buy the things I wanted, like pizza. I didn't like having to make my own dinner and then clean up the dishes every night, so whenever I had a few bucks, I'd order from Domino's and hide the cardboard evidence in the dumpster out back. I got away with that for months.

One Saturday night my mom thought she'd treat us to something special by ordering Domino's for all of us. When she called and gave the guy our address, he said, "Oh, is this for Devon?"

"Devon? My son? He's in fifth grade. How do you know Devon?" she asked.

She quickly figured out I was a regular customer, and she couldn't believe I'd been spending money ordering Dominos all the time. She got real angry about it, but she somehow didn't put together exactly where I'd been getting the money to buy all those pizzas. She thought it was from an entrepreneurial project we'd been doing at school. One of my classes allowed us to bring in things to sell, so we'd freeze some icy pops or bring in cookies. Some kids got real innovative and brought in video games and charged other kids a few dollars to play for ten minutes. But there was no way I could have earned enough money in that school project to pay for all of those pizzas, and she seemed to ignore that fact. Instead, she complained to my father, who punished me, and then to her mom, my grandmother, who took me to church on Sunday to try to set me right.

Neither of my parents were churchgoers, even though they both believe in a higher power. But my mom's mom believed the answers to just about everything could be found in the preaching she heard at her Baptist church. She was the kind of believer who thought the static on her TV was caused by the devil, and she wanted us kids to have the fear of God put into us too. So, in addition to carting us off to her Baptist church every Sunday at that point, she signed us up for the church choir—figuring that would get us in the building during the week for practices. It all felt like some sort of a punishment. And because it felt like a punishment, I didn't pay much attention to the minister's teachings or the words found on the pages of the hymnal. I was too angry and stubborn, and being angry and stubborn is like putting thick cotton balls in your ears. I was convinced it was a waste of time, and I didn't want to hear anything that would make me change my ways.

I only wanted to hear what I wanted to hear, and weirdly enough, the words and signals I kept hearing and seeing all around me seemed to encourage me to keep doing what I was doing. One day I got so bold that I broke into somebody's house—this was still when I was in the fifth grade—and stole some money and other things from that house without even thinking about it. When I didn't get caught, I took that as a sign that it was no big deal.

At some point that year my mom got a new boyfriend. He was there one night when I started complaining that my old bike was broken down and didn't have a seat anymore, and while my mom said she couldn't afford to get me a new one, that boyfriend said, "When I was a kid, we used to just steal the bike parts we needed from other bikes on the bike rack!"

*Huh*, I thought. *There's a bike rack full of good-looking bikes outside of my school every day.*

So, a couple of days later I came out the back door of Claymont Elementary, found a red bike on the rack that wasn't locked up, and told the other kids who were standing around, "Man, if I take this bike, don't say anything."

They were all supportive, like, "Alright, we won't say anything!" So I hopped on that bike and pedaled as fast as I could back to my neighborhood.

I felt all proud of myself, and I was pedaling around just playing on this new bike of mine that afternoon, when all of a sudden I looked down the street and saw a big man in a wifebeater, jean shorts, high socks, and black shoes walking toward me. I knew it could only be one man: my dad. He was fuming. I took off as fast as I could and I got away from him for a while, but at some point he caught up with me—and he gave me a beating like I'd never experienced.

That made me angry. What did my parents expect me to do? I needed a bike! All of my friends had bikes. My friends rocked Jordans and wore the latest clothes, too, and I wanted those things. It wasn't my fault if my parents were "low on cash." How else could I get what I wanted if I didn't keep doing what I was doing?

The next morning, my dad showed up at my mom's.

"Get dressed," he told me. His face was stern and his eyes were all steely. "You're in big trouble."

There was a nervousness in his voice, too, like something was wrong.

"The school found out about you stealing that bike," he said, "and they called the police, Devon. The *police*. I have to take you down to the station. Right now."

"But I gave the bike back!" I said. "I gave it back!"

"It don't matter, son. You stole it. And now you got to pay."

I was petrified. What did he mean by "pay"? Was I going to jail? I sat in the old Buick as we pulled out of the neighborhood, not knowing what was going to happen next. I'd never gotten caught for anything like this, and never even imagined that someone would call the police on me. Did one of my friends rat me out? How could they do that? And what did it matter? It was just a bike. I didn't think stealing a bike would be such a big deal.

A few minutes later my dad pulled into the parking lot of this little brick building on the side of the busy Philadelphia Pike. We walked up the granite ramp, past a marker on the building that said "1916," and into a claustrophobic lobby with a scuffed-up white tile floor. A state trooper in a blue uniform sat at the counter behind what looked like bulletproof glass.

"Can I help you?" he said.

"Yes, officer," my dad said. "This here's Devon Still, the boy we spoke about this morning. The one who stole the bike."

"Ah. Okay. Have a seat," the officer said. "The sergeant will be right with you."

I sat there staring at the floor, refusing to believe that this was really happening. I was too young to know that underage offenders weren't hauled off and put into jail. All of a sudden I heard the door handle turn, and this tall white officer with black hair stepped in.

"Devon?" he said.

"Yes," I responded.

"Come with me."

I looked at my dad, hoping he'd say something and somehow get me out of this, but he just looked at me with disappointment and sadness and motioned toward the officer with his head, like, "Go!"

"You're his father?" the officer asked my dad in a deep, stern voice.

"Yes."

"We'll get him processed and be in touch this afternoon," he said.

This giant of a man then led me inside and let the door slam shut behind me. I turned to look back, but the window in the door was too high. My dad was gone. I was alone now with this hulking white officer in a hallway with no other windows.

"This way," he said, leading me past a bunch of old portraits of policemen from prior decades and down a set of stairs into the creepy looking basement. The paint on the walls was gray and almost turned green under the flickering, discolored fluorescent lights on the ceiling. It smelled old and musty. He brought me into an even more claustrophobic room and told me that this was where I was going to get fingerprinted.

Then he pulled out a pair of gloves.

"Do you know why I'm putting on gloves?" he asked me.

"Yeah," I said. "I know. Because you don't wanna get your fingerprints on here while you're fingerprinting me."

"No," he said. "I wear gloves because I don't like touching criminals."

That hit me in my heart.

Is that what I was? A *criminal*?

He rolled my fingers one by one in the pad of black ink and then rolled them one by one into little marked boxes on a white sheet of paper.

"Just so you know," he said, "these will be scanned into the computer. We'll have these prints in the system, so if you ever commit a crime again, anywhere in the country, we'll know you did it." That cop had me convinced that my crime of stealing a bike would haunt me forever. Like it was going on my permanent record or something.

He handed me a paper towel, and I wiped the ink off of my fingers, and then he walked me across the hall to this jail cell that was tucked into a dark corner behind the stairs. There were no windows. It felt like there was no air. He told me to step inside, and I did. It was so narrow I could've reached my arms out and touched the front and back walls of that cell at the same time. It couldn't have been ten feet long from side to side, either. My heart started pounding real hard, and I felt like I couldn't breathe. There was a hard metal bench on the back wall, or maybe it was supposed to be the bed, and it was attached to the concrete with big bolts. There was a stainless-steel toilet-sink combo bolted to that same wall too. I'd never seen a toilet-sink combo before. It seemed wrong. How can you go to the bathroom and wash your hands in the same thing? And there was no privacy. No door or stall or anything. The toilet was just sitting there out in the open, visible to anyone who might come along and look between the thick, green metal bars that made up most of the outside wall.

I turned around just as the officer slid the steel-bar door closed with a *clang* and *bang* that scared me half to death. He turned around and left without saying another word. I watched his black boots as he climbed up the stairs. I grabbed onto the bars, craning my neck to try to see where he went, and to see if anyone else was around.

There was no one.

I didn't know exactly what I was charged with, or how long they planned on keeping me in that cell, or if they'd be taking me to see a judge. Nothing.

I sat down on the metal bench and felt the coldness of it. The hardness. I wondered how anybody could possibly sleep on that thing. I got real scared that this place was where I'd be spending the night, and maybe the next night, and the next.

It suddenly hit me that there was a possibility this was it. That life as I knew it was over. That waking up in the morning and seeing my mom and my brother and my sister was done now. That going to school, seeing my friends, playing basketball, playing football, having my dad around when I needed him—that might be all gone too.

What had I done? Had I just thrown my whole life away? Over a bike?

I didn't wear a watch back then, so I had no idea how long I was in there. I occasionally heard footsteps and muffled voices upstairs, but none of them ever came my way. I wasn't sure if I wanted them to. What if they came and cuffed me and took me in front of a judge? What if they sent me to an actual prison? Everyone talked about kids going to "juvie" in those days. What did that mean? Is that where I was headed? What would my mom think? Would I see my mom again? Would she have to come visit me behind bars?

An hour went by. Maybe two. Every minute, every second in that musty, dark cell, I felt scared, petrified even, and crushed by the weight of the fear of the unknown. I had messed up and messed up big-time.

I didn't think going to church with my grandmother had sunk in, and I certainly wasn't into prayer back then, but I found myself praying, or at least talking to myself, or talking to God in my head, begging Him, "God, please, please get me out of here. I'll be better. I promise. I'll *do* better. I swear! I'll do right from now on, just like mom and dad taught me. I promise. I will, I swear! Please, just get me out!"

Finally, after two or three agonizing hours, I heard footsteps coming down the stairs. I sat up. I saw the black boots. The same giant, black-haired white officer who'd locked me up walked over with a set of keys and unlocked my cell door. I stayed on the bench as the door slid open. I didn't move. I was scared that this was about to get worse.

"Stand up, boy," he said. "You're free to go."

I stood and cautiously stepped out.

"Your father's upstairs. Go on now," he said. "And don't let me see you back here."

"You won't!" I said.

I ran up those stairs as fast as I could. I got to the top and turned left down the hall, past the old photos, and when I tried to turn the door handle into the lobby it was locked. I kept trying to turn it, until all of a sudden the officer was right there next to me again. He unlocked it and opened it, and I stepped through the door into the lobby—where my dad stood there looking at me like I was nothing but a big disappointment. That look of his stung. I froze.

The lobby door slammed shut behind me and startled me, and I almost started crying, but I held it in.

"Come on," my dad said, putting his right hand on the door

handle that led to the outside world. "Thank you, officer," he said to the man behind the glass as he put his left hand on my shoulder and led me on out.

My dad didn't say anything as we walked down the ramp and got into the car. He didn't even say anything as we backed out of the parking lot. I found myself staring at the floor mat, unable to look at him, until somewhere a mile or so down the Philadelphia Pike I finally asked him in this little voice, "So . . . what happens now?"

"What happens now?" he said. "Hopefully nothing. Hopefully you learned a lesson. I had to talk them into letting you go, son. I begged and pleaded for you to get released without having to go in front of a judge. You could have been locked up in juvie for a good long time for what you did. How do you feel about that, Devon?"

"Terrible," I whispered.

"What?"

"Terrible," I said a little louder.

"You'd better feel terrible, and I'd better never catch you doing something like this again," my dad said.

"You won't," I said.

"Say what, now?"

"You won't!" I yelled.

My dad stopped talking after that. We rode in silence in the Buick. He dropped me off at my mom's, and I got out of the car without a word, knowing the promise I'd just made to him was the God's-honest truth. Spending a couple hours in that musty basement jail cell was enough of a wake-up call for me to change my ways. I was sure of it. There was no way I was going to go forward in life being labeled a "criminal." Sitting behind those bars made me feel like an animal, and I knew in my heart that no parent or police officer was going to have to remind me of that. I never wanted to feel that way again. Ever.

Getting locked up that day was enough to scare me straight.

As I lay in my bed that night, appreciating the comfort of my mattress and the warmth of my blankets for maybe the first time ever, I realized how lucky I was. I was lucky to have a mom who worked so hard to buy me those things I had. I was lucky enough to have a father who cared about me and worked hard to teach me right from wrong. A lot of kids I knew didn't have fathers around. Some didn't even know their fathers. My parents were divorced, and yet my dad was still in my life. I recognized what a gift that was, even at that young age.

So that night, even though I didn't really have a relationship with God or have any understanding of what I was doing, I thanked God for both of those two big blessings in my life. My mom and my dad.

I don't know if many kids do that. I certainly hadn't done it before that moment. I don't think I had given any real thought or appreciation to just how big of a blessing it was to have my mom and my dad in my life. I loved them, of course, but I was angry at them for messing up their marriage and messing up my life. I let my anger get in the way of seeing what I truly had, and I'm not sure if I ever would have changed if I didn't get caught for stealing that bike and those cops hadn't locked me up.

Not that I was thankful for getting locked up. I wasn't that mature and wise. Not yet, anyway. I was angry about it at the very same time I was feeling thankful for the presence of my parents.

So on that night, I just thanked God for getting me *out* of that jail cell.

I thanked God for giving me another chance.

And I promised to stop stealing. Period.

At the time, I had no idea why those officers had decided to let me go, but to my young mind, it felt like some sort of miracle. I kept going over and over it in my head, wondering what in the world my dad could've said to convince them to set me free—and wondering what would've happened to me if my dad hadn't been there to do that.

At ten years old, all I knew was that he *was* there for me. And I owed him for that.

# CHAPTER THREE

# KICKOFF

>> Turns out I owed my dad for a lot of things.

During those grammar-school and middle-school years, he kept going above and beyond in all sorts of ways to make sure us kids didn't go down the wrong path or suffer more than we had to just because he and my mom didn't get along. For example, when my mom was having trouble getting to both of her jobs on time because she didn't have a car, he gave her his Buick. He just gave it to her and went without a car for a couple of years. He woke up every day and had to take two different buses to get to work himself, but he felt like my mom needed that car more than he did because she was the one taking care of us.

How many dads would do that?

When I played my first basketball game on my sixth-grade team, my dad came through on that promise he'd made me in fourth grade— and it turned into a better reality than I'd even imagined. *Both* of my parents came to my basketball game to watch me play. Both of them. My mom *and* my dad. They sat together in the bleachers and cheered me on. I can't even begin to explain what it meant to see the two of them together after all that time apart, knowing that they were both there for me, even if it was only for an hour.

The two of them, independently, vowed that they would always be there for my games, and they were. They showed up for my first basketball game, and the next one, and the next one after that. They didn't hang around together afterward. They weren't affectionate. It didn't seem like they were going to get back together or anything like that. But they were all smiles about seeing me play, and just seeing them in the same place not yelling at each other and not angry at me—if that wasn't enough motivation to keep me playing sports, I don't know what else could be.

I knew for sure that I would keep playing *something* as long as that promise of seeing both of my parents together at my games remained a possibility.

Then in the middle of my sixth-grade year, when my mom lost one of her jobs and wasn't making enough money to afford her apartment anymore, my dad did something I still can't get over: he let my mom and us three kids move back into his apartment. He didn't get back together with my mom or anything like that. They were both still dating other people. He just let us all move in because he felt like it was the right thing to do. I didn't think of it as that big of a deal back then, but now that I'm grown and I've been through relationships and breakups of my own, I understand how hard that must have been.

"It was all for you kids," he says whenever I try to ask him about it. "I didn't want to see you kids suffer just because your mom was suffering. That's all."

That's all.

Both my dad and mom had made promises before we were even born that they would always be there for us, no matter what, and they both followed through. Somehow they managed to find the strength to work it out, to be there for us, no matter how hard it was for them.

But I didn't understand that at the time. In fact, I kept getting frustrated with my mom *and* my dad after we all were living in the same house again. My dad's new place was a few blocks south of Kynlyn Drive, on Clayton Court, and on most days after school and especially at night, they wouldn't let us out of the house.

I couldn't understand it at first, and I would fuss and complain. But remember when I mentioned that I was unaware of just how rough a place Wilmington was even a few blocks south of where we spent my early childhood years? Well, that few blocks south is exactly where we now lived.

My brother and sister and I learned real quick there were drug dealers in one of the houses across the street, and the guys who were standing around on the corners and messing around in those streets weren't playing games. They were dealing, and they were carrying. The three of us understood just as quick that our parents weren't going to let us get messed up in any of that stuff, even if it was right there on our block. That meant we were to come straight home from school and not go outside. At all. It felt like I was in jail again, except this time my cell was in my own home. We were locked inside so much that our friends started calling our house "Gander Hill," which was the name of a nearby prison.

After a few months, my mom saved up enough money to move out again, but all she could afford was a tiny apartment. So they decided we would stay with my dad. My little sister eventually moved in with my mom, but my brother and I wound up staying with my dad for the rest of our school years.

Mom knew we needed discipline, and she wouldn't be home enough working two jobs, so dad started shouldering most of the parenting duties starting in my seventh- and eighth-grade years.

My mom kept the car when she left, and it was close to a year before my dad got another car of his own, so in the interim he either walked or took the bus wherever he went. That included trips to the laundromat.

My brother and I were both big, and we both played sports, and between us and our little sister we produced a lot of laundry. I'm talking two huge industrial-sized bags full of laundry every week. Which meant my dad had to walk all the way to the laundromat with two industrial-sized bags over his shoulders.

My dad was so concerned about sheltering us from the bad influences in our neighborhood that he wouldn't even let us walk with him up the street to the laundromat to help him. He did it all by himself. And that walk was no joke. Boulevard Self-Service Laundry wasn't on our block. It wasn't even in our neighborhood. It was up a hill and around a corner, then a full *mile* down Brandywine Boulevard. That's like a twenty-minute walk each way even without pounds of laundry on your back. It would take him most of a whole day to get it washed, dried, and folded, and then he'd have to carry it all the way home.

He was shouldering a lot. We weren't little boys anymore. We were big boys who ate everything in the house and made a mess of everything in the house. Even when he got his own car and was able to take us with him to help with the laundry, it still took all day—and my brother and I complained the whole time. We hated it. We had been spoiled by our mother's lack of chore lists, apparently, and he figured he needed to find a way to keep us out of trouble and maybe teach us a few lessons while we were at it. So he made us do the work. And as fate would have it, those trips to the laundromat provided some unexpected help to him when it came to raising us boys right.

One day in between my seventh- and eighth-grade years, while he was busy washing and folding, my dad struck up a conversation with a man who happened to run an inner-city youth football team called the Raiders. Kerry Galloway, or Coach Kerry as everyone called him, was a volunteer coach who made it his mission to use football as a tool to teach young men about life, and my dad could not have met him at a better moment. He came home raving about this coach he'd met and insisting that he was gonna let us play football after school in the fall—but only if we got our grades up.

My brother and I were thrilled. We were just happy to do anything that would keep us out of Gander Hill. So we both started the school year with our heads in our books, and as soon as we brought home a few good grades on papers and tests, Dad signed us up to play on Coach Kerry's team.

That meant every day after school, instead of going to the cell of our locked-down home in our sketchy neighborhood, my brother and I hoofed it over to the football field at P. S. duPont High School. It was the first time I can remember that a coach became more than a coach to me. He pushed us on the field and pushed us to get the most out of life. He made it clear he wanted us to grow up to be great men. To think bigger. To get out of the chaos of the crazy environment we were growing up in, which I still didn't fully comprehend because of my father's protectiveness. Instead of forcing those thoughts down our throats, instead of preaching or teaching in some boring way we wouldn't listen to, he managed to get his point across by mixing all sorts of his sports lessons with life lessons, as if they were one and the same.

It turned out I was pretty good at football. I had grown a lot taller and slimmer since my elementary school days, and Coach Kerry said he saw something in me. Compared to most of my peers, he said, I now had the size and speed and some raw talent that gave me a leg up in the sport. He believed in me.

The thing that was most impressive, though, was that he seemed to believe in all of us. And that made us all work together. It was the first time I really understood what it meant for a team to play as one.

By the end of that season, we were good. We were so good we made it to the championship against the Bulldogs, a team with a star quarterback who at thirteen years old threw with the precision of a college player. His name was Charlie, and just seeing him throw passes during warm-ups made me wonder how we could possibly beat that team. Our quarterback was good, but not *that* good!

What I quickly learned over the course of that championship

game is that a single star player can't compare to the power of a unified team. Me and my fellow Raiders were unified under Coach Kerry. As a team, our whole was greater than the sum of its parts. We played our butts off, and we beat Charlie and the Bulldogs by fourteen points.

After a season of learning and trying and working harder than I'd ever worked at any sport, it all came down to one day. And on that day, I learned what it felt like to be the best. To be a champion.

Coach Kerry was responsible for teaching me that feeling.

And I liked that feeling.

What I didn't realize is that other people like that feeling too. There were coaches and scouts from some of the local high schools who came to that game and were impressed by what they saw. People who wanted to bring a piece of that championship spirit to their schools. My dad started getting calls from some of those coaches, including the receivers' coach from Howard High School.

Howard had a good football program. They had a good basketball program too. But what really appealed to my dad was the fact that Howard was a technical school, a trade school, a place that prepared kids for real-life jobs in the real world: nursing, construction, computer technology, finance. They offered a program in engine technology too. I was kind of into cars and thought that might be something cool to pursue. But there was a catch: we had to apply to get into that high school. It wasn't an automatic thing. I thought for sure that my grades weren't good enough to get me into that school, so I didn't get my hopes up.

I suppose that's that first time I learned that playing sports had added benefits. My grades might not have been the best, but the endorsement from that receivers' coach who saw me play for the Raiders was enough to put my application over the top. I got into Howard—one of the best schools in the whole city.

• • •

Guess who else got into Howard?

Charlie, the star quarterback for the Bulldogs. He and I met up on the field the first day of training camp right before freshman year, and the two of us became best friends pretty much instantly. On top of being a great athlete, Charlie was funny—and driven. He wanted to be a great football player, and he worked at it. I liked that. He had all kinds of charisma, too, like a lot of quarterbacks in the NFL seemed to have. He just seemed like a good guy, and I liked hanging around him.

My older brother got into Howard too. He was a year ahead of me in school, but with my parents' help he transferred over to Howard in his sophomore year. And another Raiders player, our buddy John, got into Howard as well. So I knew I had three good players on my football team right from the start. I was sure it was gonna be a fun year. But that's all I thought. I wasn't thinking any bigger than that at fourteen years old.

On the bus ride to Howard High, there's a sign on the side of the road that says, "Welcome to Wilmington: A place to be somebody," and I'd shake my head every time I saw it. The Wilmington I knew wasn't a place where people grow up thinking they can "be somebody." The Wilmington I knew was a place where people struggled just to survive, and that reality was about to become more clear to me than ever.

As I headed into that football season, my dad loosened the reins a little bit. He figured my brother and I wouldn't know how to handle real life if we never experienced it firsthand, and since we were old enough and big enough to get recruited for playing high school football, he figured it was probably safe to let us out of the house once in a while so we could hang out with our friends. He was still strict. "If you don't get good grades there'll be no more football and no more fooling around," he told us. He made it very clear that he expected to see my grades improve now that I was headed into high school or he'd pull me out of football and everything else.

But he gave us a little room to grow in the meantime, which let us see firsthand just how much he'd been shielding us from in our hometown.

The reality was that every time we went out to go have fun, there was a chance we might not make it home.

Someone got shot at the very first party I ever went to. It happened at the end of the night, at "the let out," when everyone spilled out into the streets. Some kid started shooting, and we all ran. I couldn't believe it was happening.

"It's no big deal," one of my brother's friends said as we caught our breath around the corner. "This always happens at the let out. Somebody starts actin' stupid and starts shootin' the joint up. Just stay out the way!"

Sometimes those shootings were purposeful—they were directed at someone specific. Other times it was just someone blowing off steam and making some noise. Either way, sometimes someone died. But it always happened. When we went to parties, we went in knowing that somebody was probably gonna get shot.

My brother and my friends and I decided from that night on never to stay until the let out. Rather than get caught up in all that, we'd try to leave parties fifteen or twenty minutes before they ended. But that strategy didn't always work, and looking back on it, I don't think it was anything but pure luck that I never got shot myself. If we'd have been smart, we would have stopped going to parties altogether. But the thing is, this was the norm. This is where we lived. You grew up knowing that one day you might be talking to your friend, and the next, his face might be on a T-shirt. That's what kids did in Wilmington when their friends got shot—they paid tribute to them by putting their picture on a T-shirt.

That was our reality. That's the life we knew. That's the life we accepted.

So, the message on that sign seemed much less real to me than another landmark we passed on the way to school every morning:

Congo Funeral Home. It was an ornate, almost castle-like gray brick building on North Market Street that seemed to run a thriving business built on Wilmington kids who never grew up to be anything but dead.

I guess it seems strange to some people that I wasn't scared of dying, but that's just what happens when you grow up like that. You go about your life knowing every time you go out might be your last. So there's no sense being scared about it. You just learn to be smart about it. You learn to watch your back and check over your shoulder. You steer clear of trouble. You cross the street if you see trouble on the sidewalk up ahead. You don't go out alone late at night. And otherwise, you just live your life.

For me, at fourteen years old, the only part of life I really liked was playing sports, so that's what I did. I played football at Howard, and I was a starter right out of the gate. I'm not sure why the coaches started me as a freshman, other than there was a lack of other talent available, because I wasn't very good. For all the promise Coach Kerry saw in me, I was completely undeveloped as a football player. Years later my friend Charlie popped in a videotape of me playing my freshman year, just for laughs. I looked so bad on the field that I ran up, hit the eject button, and broke the tape because I never wanted anyone to see the evidence of just how bad I was!

Although football had been my ticket to Howard High, my mind was still on the basketball court. As football season came to an end, I started playing AAU basketball right away, and I played hard. In AAU we might play five games a day, and I loved it. But there were a lot of days when I could only play one game because my knees hurt so bad. I'd wind up benched with ice packs all the time, and I had no idea why. The coaches and doctors and even my dad assumed it was just because I was growing so fast.

"It's growing pains, son. You'll get over it," they'd say. "Ice it up and get back out there!"

It was frustrating not being able to play every game, but the pain was real. It seemed to me that pain was just a part of playing sports, and if I wanted to get in the game, I needed to push through it. So that's what I did. No matter how much I was hurting, I never missed game day, and I never missed a single practice—well, except for one.

At the end of my first quarter of high school, we all gathered in an assembly so that our teachers could pass out our report cards. I was all kinds of nervous. I had my dad's voice ringing in my ears, and I knew that if my grades weren't good, I could kiss football and basketball and going to parties goodbye. I'd always struggled with my grades, but I was so into sports now that I worked extra hard in the classroom just because I didn't want to lose what I loved. I hoped it had paid off, but I truly didn't know what my final grades were going to be.

When a teacher came around and handed me a report card, the first thing I noticed was that it said "Honor Roll" at the top. I thought maybe they'd given me somebody else's report card by mistake. But sure enough, that report card had my name on it. I couldn't believe it. I'd never made honor roll in my life.

I went sprinting out to the bus after school. The buses drove right past the practice fields, so I ducked down in my seat to make sure the coaches didn't see me trying to leave. To me, skipping practice was worth it. I went home to show my dad that report card, and he was so happy. "I'm so proud of you, Devon!" he said. "You keep this up and you're going to college. You'll write your ticket to anywhere you want to go. Anything you want to do!"

I wasn't thinking about college, and I didn't know anything I wanted to do other than hang out with my friends, but I soon learned that getting on the honor roll was a game changer. It gave my dad a whole new confidence in me. That was all it took, and my strict dad started saying "yes" to whatever I wanted.

"Can I go to the movies tonight?"

"Sure!"

"Can I go over my friend's house after school?"

"No problem, Devon. Just don't be home late. It's a school night."

"Can we go out to eat tonight?"

"Why not? Where you want to go?"

That report card changed everything, and I decided that no matter what it took, I would stay on the honor roll for the rest of my school years. I mean, why wouldn't I want to do the work it took to make my life easier and more fun?

Not long after that report card came out, high school basketball season started, and I felt like I was on a roll. Before I knew it, I was headed into January thinking I didn't need to make myself a New Year's resolution because life was already good.

Then at practice one day we got into a layup line, and after a couple of times through, everyone in front of me started trying to go up and dunk. I wasn't the tallest guy on the team, and I'd never really tried to dunk before, but when I saw all the upperclassmen dunking, I decided to give it a shot.

Big mistake.

The next thing I remember, I woke up flat on the ground. Everyone was gathered all around me looking real worried. "You okay? You okay, man?" they said, all hushed. I realized I was unable to move. I looked down and saw that my shinbone was cracked in two. The bottom of my leg was all bent, as if I had another knee in the middle of my tibia or something. Suddenly the pain hit me, searing and sharp, the way I imagined a bullet must feel, only bigger. This was more like a cannonball had shattered my leg.

"What happened?" I yelled, bending at my waist and trying to grasp my leg.

"When you came down under the rim, your leg just snapped, man," someone said. "Right in half," someone added. "You passed out." "Just like that." "You went down *hard*."

In a matter of minutes, the site of the break swelled up the size of a basketball. The pain was unbearable. The coaches seemed like they couldn't decide what to do about it. For some reason they didn't want to call an ambulance. So instead, they called my dad.

It felt like it took forever for him to get there, and when he finally did it seemed like the whole team tried to carry me out to his car and slide me into the back seat. Without a stretcher, they couldn't do it. There wasn't enough room in there for my stretched out six-foot-two body anyway—which meant I had to bend. I had to sit on the back seat and turn and lift my dangling broken leg up into the car. The pain was horrendous. When somebody slammed the door shut I almost blacked out again.

Everything moved real fast after that. The streets went by in a blur as white-hot pain seared through my leg. It throbbed and burned as every pothole rattled through me. When we got to the hospital, they took me right in, and the doctors discussed everything with my dad. I heard him tell them that I was a good athlete, so they needed to do a good job or my future was over.

Their biggest fear was that my growth plate was broken. If that was the case, they'd have to go into my other leg and break the growth plate there, too, which meant I wouldn't grow anymore. I wouldn't get any taller. I couldn't believe what I was hearing.

Next thing I knew my dad was saying, "I love you, son. Be strong. Be *strong*!" and the nurses started wheeling me down a hallway into surgery.

I kept thinking, *Why did this happen? Why?*

As the anesthesiologist put a mask over my nose and told me to count backwards from a hundred, I got real worried. *What if this means I can't ever play basketball again?*

I felt nauseous. I wanted to vomit. I started feeling sleepy. *What's gonna happen to me? God, what's gonna happen to me?*

# CHAPTER FOUR

# FIRST DOWN

>> Seven hours later I woke up in a fog. I opened my eyes and saw both of my parents right there with me, one on each side of the bed.

"You did good, Devon," my mom said. "The doctors say you're gonna be fine."

"You're gonna be more than fine," my dad said. "The doctors said the surgery went real well. You're gonna be in a cast for a while, and definitely have some physical therapy to go through, but they said you'll be able to play basketball and football again and be good as new in no time."

I didn't say much. I was still stunned by the whole thing. Depressed, even. I didn't understand how something like that could happen. How did my leg just bust in half? I still don't understand it to this day. The doctors said there wasn't any real reason for it. It was just a freak accident.

They put me in a cast that stretched all the way from my toes to my hip, and despite what my dad said, I lay there thinking to myself that there was no way I'd ever be able to play football again. There was no way I'd ever be able to dunk a ball again. I looked at that giant cast and thought, *My sports career is over.*

Then something really strange happened. A doctor came in. A white woman who'd worked on my surgery. She was wearing blue scrubs, with a scrub hat that tied in the back over her blonde hair, like she'd just walked out of the operating room. She must've been in her late thirties or early forties, and she asked me how I was doing. "Fine," I said. I'm sure my face said otherwise. I don't think I could even muster a smile at that point.

"Are you in pain?" she asked.

"Nah," I said.

I was lying. It hurt like hell.

"Well that's good," she said. "Hey, you should check to see if anyone's signed your cast yet."

As she walked out of the room I pulled the blanket up, and sure enough there was a message on my cast. I couldn't bend far enough to see what she wrote, so I asked my mom to read it to me.

"It's from her. It says, 'You're going to be somebody special when you grow up,'" my mom said. She looked over at me and then looked at my dad, then back at me. "Wow," she said. "Ain't that something?"

It caught me off guard. I had no idea why that doctor would write that on my cast. She didn't even know me. But for some reason, I couldn't stop thinking about it. I never saw her again, but I remember her face to this day.

"You're going to be someone special when you grow up."

The power of that woman's words resonated through me as I dozed off again.

I wish I'd thought to keep that part of the cast when it finally came off. I feel like her words should be hanging on a wall somewhere. But that cast didn't come off for quite a while, and once it did, I think I was just glad to see it thrown in the garbage.

When I got out of the hospital, I spent a whole week at my

mom's apartment. The doctor's orders said to rest and not push myself. Staying at her place made sense because my mom worked down the street, which meant she could come check on me during the day. But I was miserable. Every day I lay in her bed crying, like, "Why did this have to happen to me?"

I didn't want to be home by myself. The isolation made me crazier than the pain did. So I started begging my mom every time she came home, "Please, please let me go back to school. I can't stand this!"

She asked my dad about it, and they thought they'd better see if I could get out of the house and move around before shipping me off on the school bus or something. The cast was huge, and I'd barely even tried to use my crutches, let alone the wheelchair they sent home for me from the hospital. So my parents decided to take me to a basketball game just to see how things went.

As soon as I came hobbling around the corner of the bleachers into the gym, somebody up in the stands spotted me, and all of a sudden the whole crowd started cheering. It was crazy. It sounded like the Wildcats had just won the championship, but all that noise was directed at *me*. My teammates ran over and started patting me on the back and trying to shake my hand. I could barely balance on my crutches at that point, but they packed so close around me, I couldn't have fallen even if I tipped right over.

I don't know why the students all started cheering me like that. I wasn't a star player. I'd barely even gotten a chance to play that season. But I guess word got around about just how scary my accident was. Maybe the story that spread made it seem like a miracle that I was up and walking back into that gym after only a couple of weeks. I'm not sure. It just felt good to see people smiling and cheering me on. For the first time in days, I didn't feel any pain. I felt something else. I felt hope and love and maybe a little "I've got this."

*Yeah*, I thought, *I definitely need to go back to school. I need this type of love every day if I'm gonna get through this!*

When I went back to my first class on Monday, I had all kinds of friends and classmates offer to help push me around in my wheelchair. I'm sure some of them were just people who wanted to get out of class a little early or something, but it didn't matter. It was fun! People connecting to me and all that laughing helped. It felt like everyone in that school suddenly knew who I was, and they had my back.

• • •

What didn't feel good, though, was my physical therapy. Two and a half months after the accident, the cast came off. That's when the hard part of my recovery began. My muscles had atrophied, and my leg was so stiff from being stuck in a bent position I needed to reteach my leg how to move.

To do that the therapists made me sit in this chair. I'll never forget *the chair.* They put another chair out in front of me and had me put my foot up on it, putting my knee sort of bent up in the air a bit between the two chairs. Then they pulled this thick, wide, black resistance band up from an anchored spot on the floor beneath my leg, and they wrapped it up over my knee and tightened it so that the tension pulled my leg toward the ground.

It was awful.

"Try not to fight it," they told me. "We'll be back in thirty minutes."

*Thirty minutes?!* For thirty minutes I sat there getting my bent knee pulled relentlessly toward the floor. It was torture. It hurt, and I hated it. When my time was up, I moaned and complained that I didn't want to go anymore, but my dad wasn't hearing it. "The pain won't last forever, son," he said. "This is only temporary. Get through this, and you'll be back on your feet in no time."

I think Dad knew I wouldn't make it through therapy on my own. So, he always went with me and sat right there through the whole thing. Every time.

Thankfully, he was right. The chair worked. After just a couple of weeks my leg got straightened out again, and the torture ended. Then we started working on rebuilding my muscles and training me to walk right again.

It was springtime and the school year was almost over by the time the physical therapy was nearing an end. I was walking again. I kept trying hard not to limp, and I could fake it pretty well in front of the therapists, just hoping that they'd finally say I was good to go and could walk out of there for good. But I was still scared. I was scared to go back to basketball. I was scared to even think about getting back on the football field, where I'd get hit and knocked down, or running or jumping in any way. Just because I was able to walk again didn't mean that my leg was up to playing sports, especially the way I liked to play them.

On what I hoped would be one of the last therapy sessions that spring, toward the end of my freshman year, the therapist took me out into a hallway.

"Head on up those stairs," he said.

It was like half a flight of stairs up to a landing that then turned to go up to the second floor. I walked up them as casual and confident looking as possible, knowing this was probably a final test to see if I'd be able to leave that place and not come back.

"Good," the therapist said as I reached the landing.

My dad was right there with us.

"Looking good, Devon," he said as I turned around and looked down at them.

"Okay," the therapist said. "Now jump."

"What?" I asked.

"Jump down," he said.

"Like, one step at a time? Or—"

"No, the whole thing. Jump all the way to the bottom."

"What do you mean, 'jump'? I just broke my leg!"

"You didn't just break it. You've spent four months healing and rebuilding your strength. Trust me. You've got this. Jump."

I could not believe what this man was asking me to do. I hadn't jumped an inch, let alone a whole flight of stairs. What if I jumped down and broke my leg again and had to start all over? I couldn't even handle the thought of that.

I looked at my dad, hoping he'd get me out of it, and my dad looked at the therapist, and the therapist nodded, like, "He's ready." So, my dad turned back to me and said, "Alright now, Devon. Do what the man says. Jump!"

If my mom had been there, I'm sure she would have talked the therapist out of it. She would have said, "Oh, my boy's not ready. Let's wait until next time." She would have done anything to keep me from worrying, and certainly from getting hurt again.

But my dad? He trusted that the therapist knew what he was doing, and he trusted that I had done the work I needed to do to heal my leg.

"You can do it," he said. "You're better now. Time to prove it to yourself."

I must've stood there for a solid ten minutes debating whether or not to actually jump. I kept getting myself ready, walking right up to the edge, even swinging my arms back—and then I'd step back again, terrified.

"Come on, Devon. You can do it!" my dad kept saying.

Finally I just held my breath and jumped.

I landed. It didn't break. It didn't even hurt.

"Yeah!" my dad yelled.

"Nice job," the therapist chimed in.

My leg was just fine. I had no idea I had come that far. In an instant, that leap gave me all the confidence in the world that I would actually be able to get back on the court and back on the field to start playing again.

With my physical therapy over, I started working out on my own, taking walks, running, jumping, making sure any sign of that injury was gone. And when training camp for football started up in late July, I was there with my team, ready to tackle the world. It would take me a full season to get back into shape. It would take me pretty much my whole sophomore year before I would get all the way back to giving it my all in every game. I didn't want to risk re-injuring myself, and that fear can block you from playing as hard as you want to. But whenever I stopped and thought about what I'd been through, I was astounded at what I'd accomplished.

In seven short months I'd gone from thinking I might never be able to play sports again to achieving what most people would consider a full recovery. Was it hard? Yes! But it wasn't *that* hard. Did it hurt? Yes! But the pain was only temporary. The pain went away. I didn't let the pain or the difficulty stop me. I didn't give up. I worked at it, and my work paid off.

The pain I experienced at the moment was far less than the pain I would've felt if I never played sports again. The pain was only temporary.

It's funny, but I knew I wasn't the most athletic person at my school. (My friends Charlie and John were far more athletic than me, and so were some of the other kids.) But after going through that injury, I knew that I had something more important. I proved to myself that I was willing to go through pain and sacrifice in order to live my dream of playing sports. I didn't give up when life threw me an obstacle. With the help of my personal support team, I persevered. And I was positive that if I ever had to do it again, I could.

If you're into sports, you hear people say things all the time like, "Yeah, I was supposed to be a pro ballplayer, but I blew my knee out, and that ended my career." The fact that I'd gone through a major leg surgery at fourteen years old and came out the other side of it playing football and basketball again gave me a whole different mindset. I felt like it wouldn't matter how many times I blew my knee out, broke a bone, or blew my back out or whatever. None of those things would be an excuse for me to stop. In fact, I started to count on the fact that other people might give up when things got hard. I started to think that maybe that would be my advantage: when other players gave up, I would be the one to take their spot and get ahead because I was willing to go through whatever it took to get there.

Breaking my leg in that freak accident was a blessing in disguise. What could have been a setback became an advantage. And that made a huge difference on my outlook for the future.

• • •

One night Charlie, Tony, John, and I went to a basketball game at a rival high school. We ran into another friend named Will while we were there. He and Charlie kept joking around all night. Will wasn't a close friend, but he was a good kid. We all liked him.

The next night, at a basketball game at our school, this girl came running up to me looking all freaked out. "Is it true?" she asked.

"Is what true?" I said.

"Is it true that Will's dead?"

"What? What are you talking about? We was just with Will last night!"

"No, they're saying he just got shot."

I called one of my friends. "Yo, did Will get killed?"

"Yeah," he said. "Will's dead."

Word was he was in the wrong place at the wrong time, and somebody came up and shot him in the back of the head. Dead. Just like that.

The fact that I'd been talking to him and my best friend, Charlie, had been joking around with him right before it happened hit me hard. It was as close as I'd come to having one of my own friends wind up on a T-shirt, and it shook me.

I didn't want to go down that way. I didn't want to get caught up in the drugs and the shootings. What was the point of it all?

What was the point of anything I'd accomplished if I was going to wind up on a T-shirt?

I'm pretty sure it was right then and there I decided to get out.

I was listening to a lot of Tupac at that time. He'd become one of my favorite artists, and he really made me feel like I could be simultaneously proud of where I was from, but also not want to stay there. His music let me know that I should never give up; that for sure there was a chance I could make it out of that situation. Tupac himself got out by using his talents—in his case, music. Maybe playing sports was mine.

A lot of people seem like they're scared of Tupac or something when they've never even listened to him. I'd sit in my room with my headphones on, listening to songs with titles like "Keep Ya Head Up." I'd been listening to Tupac since the sixth grade. My parents would buy me his CDs for birthdays and holidays. And after Will's death, the messages of that music were a big part of what made me decide to double down on the path I was on and see where it led me.

My parents and coaches kept talking to my brother and me about going to college on a football scholarship, but I had never even seen a college. I didn't know what it was all about, other than the fact that they had real nice stadiums that I saw on TV when I watched games with my dad. I knew college cost a lot of money, and my parents didn't have a lot of money. And even though people kept talking about scholarships, I had no idea how someone might go about getting one. I hoped I could do it. I wished I could go to college. But it was hard to imagine how it was really gonna happen.

My ability to see that future grew even cloudier because it looked like my older brother wasn't going to make it. He wasn't going to be allowed to play football his senior year. He'd stayed back in the ninth grade before he transferred to Howard, and the rules of high school sports said he could only play for four years. Not playing at all that year would likely blow his chances at a scholarship, and my parents didn't want to see that happen. He was a talented athlete, and my parents were sure he'd have a shot at a scholarship if he played. So they got together with the superintendent and the coaches and some of Tony's teachers, and they decided to take his case to the Delaware Board of Sports to ask for a second chance. My parents wanted them to allow Tony to stay as a fifth-year senior and play football again.

The powers that be made it clear to my parents there was almost no chance they'd succeed, because they couldn't go around giving every kid a second chance. But my mom went in there, and she was passionate. She championed his case and caused them to change their minds.

By using the power of her words, and by blaming herself for his need for extra time, she got that board to believe in her son's ambition to do better; in his ability to play football, to go to college, and to make something of himself. She convinced them he would follow through. She never had a chance to do that herself, so she fought for him. Mom's commitment was always to see that we got our best chance at getting a good education.

I was blown away. In my teen years I had spent most of my time with my dad. He was the one who seemed to make the most sacrifice in order to raise us. He was the one who was usually there whenever we were in trouble, either to set us straight or to give us the moral support we needed. But when my mom did that for my brother, I saw her in a whole new light.

I remember looking at her and thinking, even then, at fifteen years old, *Man, if you're willing to go that far, I know what type of parent I need to be when I grow up.*

My brother took that second chance and ran with it like he'd just been reborn. He got his grades up. He never missed a practice. He wound up having his best year ever on the football field, and sure enough, before football season was out, he had a partial scholarship offer in hand from Carson-Newman University, a Christian liberal arts college in Tennessee. It was a smaller school, but their athletic program had produced 269 All-Americans, 6 team national championships, and too many conference titles to count. It blew my mind to think that my brother had earned a scholarship to go to a place like that!

Seeing all of that unfold, seeing what my parents did for Tony and how much more focused he was once he knew he had a second chance in life, it felt like I'd been given my own second chance at life too. It felt like someone had lit a fire under me. I suddenly wanted to get up and get going every day. I wanted to do my best every day. I wanted to prove to my coaches and classmates that I was worthy of that applause they gave me when I came back after my injury. I wanted to prove that I was an asset to Howard High School's football program, basketball program, track team, everything! I wanted to prove I was an academic asset, too, and I spent all sorts of extra hours in the engine technology classroom doing extra-credit work, just so I'd stand out as a student. I wanted to get myself on a college-scholarship track as soon as possible *without* having to stay for a fifth year or force my mom to make another plea to some board. I started training harder, and studying harder, and working out harder every day. Even in summer.

It was over the course of my sophomore year, though, that I realized not all of those sports I was into were meant for me. By the time the year was over, I was six foot five, solid as a rock, and pretty much just too big to accomplish the kind of success I wanted on the basketball court or in track and field. But with all that growth combined with all my new drive, and all the fresh confidence I had in my ability to persevere, I still had one obvious place to shine: on the football field.

Most of my friends played football too. I was hanging around a group of guys who slept, ate, and breathed football, so I joined them in that pursuit. I let football consume my life. Even before training camp started, we got together every single day and started working out. We would go to the field and run our own drills. Most of my friends weren't linemen like me; they were receivers and defensive backs who spent a lot of their time doing footwork and working on speed. I did those drills right alongside them, and that started to set me apart from my peers on the defensive line. Those footwork drills made me quicker than my peers. My coaches and other observers started calling me the fastest lineman in the whole state, and I know that wasn't because of my natural athleticism or size. It was because of the extra work I did and the dedication I showed and my persistence in getting out there every day and doing those footwork drills, in addition to the standard work I did on the line.

If the weight room opened up after school at 3:00 p.m., me and my friends would be there pounding on the door at 2:30 trying to get in. The coaches saw our drive and pulled us away from the weights sometimes. They made us play dodgeball with volleyballs, anything they could think of to push us a little harder and make us a little quicker. We spent so much time there, I wouldn't be surprised if once in a while they tried to run us ragged just to wear us out so we'd go home.

• • •

That dedication didn't leave us a whole lot of free time to mess around with partying or getting into trouble. But it left *some* time. And trouble seems to have a way of finding kids whether they're looking for it or not.

For all the drugs I saw and managed to avoid in my own neighborhood, and right in my own school, the only time I tried smoking pot was when I went up to Camden on a couple of weekends and hung out with my cousins. I never really got high because I didn't know how to smoke, and it wasn't something I was interested in doing. But I tried it anyway. And that made it easier later on, when the opportunity came to try it again.

At home, I wound up at parties almost every weekend. It's hard not to feel bored and want to do something fun when you're a teenager with all kinds of energy, and you're out looking at girls who are now looking at you because you're an athlete.

One time, just after a party let out, I noticed a black female cop walking the sidewalk, keeping an eye on all of us as we spilled into the streets. Then the craziest thing happened. Somebody came out of the party, right in front of me, and pulled out a gun. He pointed it toward the sky, and he fired it into the air.

The cop didn't do anything. She just looked at the kid and shook her head.

It was crazy!

Why I was there, I don't know. Why I didn't steer entirely clear of parties when I knew what I really wanted was to get out and go to college, I don't know. But those sorts of near misses with Will and that kid firing a gun into the air between me and that cop— these things just kept happening. And I kept blowing them off as if they were no big deal, when I should have been heeding them as warning shots.

CHAPTER FIVE

# FIELD GOAL

>> For those of us who were dedicated to it, sports are what saved us from the city. Sports wouldn't save us from everything, though. In time, we'd learn that the hard way.

It was the summer after my sophomore year. Our head coach, Coach Ritter, decided to take our team to a training camp in West Virginia before our preseason practices started at home. And in the middle of planning for the trip, I received my first scholarship offer.

Marshall University reached out to Coach Ritter by email and asked him to send me their way. Based on what they'd seen already, before I'd even reached my junior year, they were prepared to make me a member of the Thundering Herd.

I was shocked. So were my parents. We didn't expect to start fielding offers for another year or two, and the offer was beyond anything I'd even dared to dream. Marshall's a Division 1 school with a long history of conference championships and a couple of national championships produced by a long list of All-Americans who went on to become NFL players, most notably Randy Moss.

The school was even known outside of the college football universe because of the 2006 film *We Are Marshall*, which starred Matthew McConaughey.

This was it. It was all happening so fast. When I started high school, I didn't even know what I was looking for or how I was gonna get out of Wilmington, but I worked hard, I did my best— and the answer came looking for me.

"Sign me up!" I told my parents.

Thankfully, they slowed me down. They told me, "Be patient." We hadn't even gone to visit the school, they reminded me. I had no idea if it was the right school for me. And I had my whole junior and senior years ahead of me.

"You keep playing like you're playing and the offer will still be there next year," my dad said. "And if you play even better, there'll be better offers."

"Better than Marshall? A D1 school?" I said.

My dad smiled and gave me a big hug. Coach Ritter confirmed that I should hold off and see what other offers came in. So I tried to be patient, and I decided to follow my father's advice and work even harder. If Marshall University was after me after just one season back from my leg injury, what sort of offers could I field if I was playing at my absolute best? What sort of offers could I get after training even harder than I already was? It was exciting.

My junior year, everything clicked. I stopped growing. My workouts and training paid off. I made thirteen sacks in a single season. That's unheard of.

Coach Ritter put a packet together to hand out to college coaches whenever he saw them at conferences. Over the course of the next few months, he made the rounds and approached a whole bunch of them and said, "Hey, I got a kid that might interest you. He's six-five. He's 250. He plays D-end." He then handed them an envelope with a DVD highlight reel of my best moments, along with a transcript showing I was an honor-roll student.

Every school he spoke to wound up calling and wanting to see me.

He made phone calls to schools on the West Coast and sent them packages too. And every one of those schools came calling. Truly, every school anyone might associate with football came after me except for three: Notre Dame, Texas, and Southern Cal.

It felt like the whole world was opening up. By the time senior year came around, there were coaches flying in just to meet with me. I was in shock about it all. I didn't quite know how to handle it. I got so quiet that as soon as I left the room some of those visiting coaches would ask Coach Ritter, "Does he talk?"

My parents both wanted me to make the right decision, so they started driving me around to visit these colleges. The NCAA only allows colleges to pay for one "official" visit with any prospective player, but my parents wanted me to really spend time at the schools and get a feel for them. So my dad, who still wasn't making very much money, somehow managed to get time off and pay for a whole bunch of "unofficial visits," which involved long car rides out to the schools I thought I was most interested in. What was even more amazing to me was that both of my parents came on most of those trips. They got past whatever differences they had and spent hours together in a car with me, just to help me make the right decision for my future. My dreams were beginning to come true.

Choosing the right school and the right scholarship was a really big deal to my dad. It turns out he had been offered a basketball scholarship himself when he was in high school. He'd never told me about it until we started looking at schools. I mentioned how much he loved the game, and how good he was at the game. I wondered why he'd never pursued it professionally, but it all started to make sense once he told me the story. Turns out his high school coach set the whole thing up for him. Since his dad wasn't in the picture, my dad didn't really have any guidance about the whole thing. So, he trusted that coach and took him at his word. My dad traveled to school that fall, only to find out that the scholarship didn't go through. He didn't have enough money to enroll in school without it, so he went back home with his dream of playing college basketball completely crushed.

There was no way he was going to let that happen to either me or Tony, so he got involved in every detail of the offers that landed on my table, while my mom dug into all the questions about the schools' academic programs, and the living arrangements, and just how well I would be taken care of when she sent her baby off into the arms of one of these programs and their coaches.

My mom and dad were still coming to all my games too. As a senior in high school, I could still look up in the stands and see both of my parents cheering for me every game. There is no doubt in my mind that having that support was a big part of my success.

I still don't know how my dad paid for all those college visits, though, especially after we made one particular trip to Tennessee. The point of the trip was to show my brother the campus of Carson-Newman, but since the University of Tennessee was close by, we decided it would be a good chance for me to tag along and take a look at that school too. For some reason my dad had to rent a car for that trip. He was real tired the night we left, so he let Tony drive, and not two minutes after we got on the highway, a big tractor trailer in front of us blew a tire off. Tony drove right over it. It messed up the whole underside of the rental car—and Dad had declined to take the insurance. The car was still okay to drive. We made it all the way to Tennessee and back. But the repairs cost a small fortune.

Still, he wasn't discouraged. He paid for every one of those trips. And every one of those trips was worth it.

Seeing all those college campuses was like waking up and putting on a new pair of glasses. It's like I'd been stuck in blinders all my life. I couldn't believe there were kids my age all over America living and studying in places that seemed like Disney World compared to Wilmington. I could hardly believe that I was going to get to live on one of those campuses, train in state-of-the-art facilities, and play in those stadiums I'd seen on TV.

Everywhere we went, people started talking to me about life beyond college, too, about me having what it takes to make it to the NFL. It was crazy. This was real, and it was crazy.

Of all the schools we visited, there was one that stood head and shoulders above the rest: Ohio State. I fell in love with the place. It's hard to explain. It was just a feeling I had. The players were fun. I felt more comfortable there than I had at any of the other schools.

I didn't let anyone except my dad know that Ohio ranked number one in my mind. I kept my decision-making close to the vest.

"There are still other schools, Devon," my dad told me. "You haven't even been to Penn State yet! You promised those coaches you would go for a visit, and a man keeps his word."

My dad just wanted me to keep my promises, but the allure of Penn State was definitely huge. Anywhere we went in our whole region, from up in Camden, to Philadelphia, all over Delaware and beyond, there were Penn State fans. Penn State's football program is legendary, and its teams had won championship after championship for decades—going all the way back to 1966—led by one of the greatest coaches in the game, Joe Paterno.

When we finally visited Penn State, I didn't get a chance to meet Joe Paterno. I met with some of the other members of his coaching staff instead, and they were great. Especially the man who would be my coach if I chose that school, Coach Johnson. He seemed like the kind of guy who was completely, 100 percent dedicated to his players. He spoke about the kind of support and training I would get in his program, and I believed him.

The campus was beautiful. Seeing the trophy case was awe-inspiring. But it was a short visit, and the place seemed so close to home that I sort of dismissed it. Ohio State was number one for me, and if I was going to go anyplace else I thought I might go to Miami, or some other place that was warm. I was tired of the cold weather in Wilmington. In my mind, thoughts of warmth and sunshine initially outranked the attraction of Penn State's impressive football history.

I think the coaches at Penn State could tell I wasn't all that into it. I guess I hardly spoke a word the whole time I was there, and they felt like they didn't get to know me at all during my visit. In my mind it didn't matter. I still wanted Ohio State.

We had coaches fly in from Michigan, Michigan State, and Oklahoma, all in one day. They were sitting on chairs outside of Coach Ritter's office like kids waiting to go see the principal, but they were all there to see me.

In the off-season, I held down a job at Finish Line, the sneaker and athletic gear store, to try to earn some honest money. One day Coach Jim Tressel from Ohio State came walking into the store with a pizza for me and my coworkers to share. He said he wanted to thank me for my time, that he appreciated my work ethic, and that he wanted to show me how much I would be taken care of if I came to his school.

It's hard not to let that kind of attention go to your head.

But things got even crazier.

We heard back from Penn State. They wanted to take another shot. Only this time, they didn't want me to come to their campus. Joe Paterno, the legend, a man who had a reputation for never traveling off campus except for games, was coming to our high school to visit me. Word was he'd seen my highlight reel and personally decided to make the trip all the way to Wilmington just to have lunch with my coaches and me.

When Joe Paterno walked through those doors, it felt like the whole world stopped and bowed down for him. The entire school was buzzing with awe and respect. He wound up signing all kinds of balls and T-shirts and gear, not only for students, but for teachers and coaches and administrators who came out of their offices and stood patiently against the walls waiting for a chance to get close to the man. The local news station came and parked their van out front with a live satellite feed to try to get a few words with him. I'd never seen anything like it.

I don't remember the specifics of what Coach Paterno said to me when we met that day. I think I was too excited to listen. All I know is that by the end of the day, he'd made an impression on me that changed everything. Joe Paterno seemed to love the game of football and to love his team's players more than any coach I'd ever met. It was like icing on the cake of the talk I'd had with Penn State's Coach Johnson, who seemed to put his players' well-being above every other measure.

By the time JoePa left, I was as awestruck as any of my class-mates and teachers. Maybe more. I *got it*. This man wasn't just a coach. He was like a father figure, an inspiration not only to his players but to tens of thousands, maybe millions of fans. He'd earned a level of respect that almost no other coach in the game had. I saw the respect he commanded up close and in person, and I suddenly understood how much support a guy like Coach Johnson would have when it came to treating his players right.

I knew right then and there, *That's who I want to play for.*

But I continued to keep my decision close to the vest. I had learned that it was in my own best interest to wait until the last second to announce my decision. The media attention would be good for my high school and for the players who came after me.

At this point I had scholarship offers on the table from more than fifty colleges and universities. My dad was just about burst-ing at the seams at the thought that *both* of his boys were going to college—and that his youngest son was about to be taken under the wings of "JoePa" Joe Paterno and the Nittany Lions.

He got teary-eyed every time we talked about it. So did I.

I was riding high, and I thought the rest of my little football crew would be too. The whole crew lived, ate, and breathed football for most of our high school years—but in the end, I was the only one of us who wound up with scholarship offers. Those guys were better athletes than me, I was sure of it. Unfortunately, I think our high school underestimated the chances some of the guys had because of their size. For example, my buddy John was small, but he was one of the quickest, most-talented runners I'd ever seen. Nobody could tackle him! But because he wasn't a big guy, it seemed like he didn't get the kind of support I did. Whatever the reason was, they were happy for me. We supported each other, and pushed each other, and all of us felt like we were on our way up, and on our way out—scholarships or not.

That attitude sort of went to our heads a little bit though. We had all sorts of attention from girls, and we got busy making the most of it. Especially John. He was definitely the ladies' man of the bunch. Charlie got himself a steady girlfriend at one point, and I sort of played the field until one day, one of the girls I had gone on a few dates with asked me if we could make it official.

I said "yes," never thinking it would last beyond high school. I didn't think that relationship was all that serious. All I knew is I was gettin' outta Wilmington. "Penn State here I come!"

• • •

With graduation around the corner, my buddies and I decided it was time to cut loose and celebrate. We heard about a big party that was happening one weekend, and we decided to go.

That party, like pretty much every other party I'd ever gone to, was a whole lot of fun—and it ended with a shooting.

I should have heeded the warning shots.

I looked over my shoulder and actually saw the guy with the gun. It was that close. It didn't look like he actually shot anybody. He missed his target. But it was loud. As soon as it happened we ran to the car, and as we were about to pull off, the shooter jumped in the car with us.

My friend started the engine and pulled away so fast that he forgot to turn his headlights on. That was the wrong thing to do. We didn't make it a quarter mile up the street before five cop cars were on us with the blues flashing. They pulled us over and boxed us in. One of them yelled over a loudspeaker, "Stay in your vehicle!"

In the headlights we could see the silhouettes of like ten cops step out of their cars, guns drawn, headed right for us. Next thing I knew, we were surrounded, and in between the flashes and darkness I realized that one of those guns was pointed directly at my face.

"Step out of the car," the cop said.

I went to reach for my seat belt, and I swear I could feel him grip that gun ten times tighter. I thought I was about to get my head blown off. I threw my hands up and looked at him, wide-eyed and terrified in the blinding light of his flashlight. "I just need to take my seat belt off!" I said.

"Do it," he said. "Just one hand. Slowly. Make sure I can see it," he said.

I clicked the button and opened the door and stepped outside with my hands up 'til the cop turned me around and pushed me against the car.

A couple of other cars full of kids from that party went screaming by, and more than one of them leaned out the window, clowning around and yelling, "Cuff 'em, officer!" or "Glad you got 'em." "That's what you get for shootin' someone!"

They cuffed us all and sat us down on the side of the road. They asked if we knew about the shooting at the party, and of course we all said, "No."

When one officer got in my face and asked me directly, I said, "What are you all talking about? I didn't do anything wrong!"

While we sat there, humiliated as even more cars drove by with kids laughing at us, the officers searched the car—and found the gun. It was still hot from being fired.

"Whose gun is this? Whose gun is it?!" the cops yelled. And none of us would give the shooter up. Coming from the environment we come from, you just don't go telling the cops who did it. There were consequences for that kind of talk. We all knew better than to say one word.

In the meantime, they pulled our IDs and got on their radios doing background checks. After a few minutes they arrested one of my friends and threw him in the back of a car. Then they came back and arrested the kid who we all knew did the shooting. Then a white cop walked up to me, and I thought for sure I was next. I could just about hear the sound of my scholarships getting flushed down the toilet. I could picture my father's face. It felt like my whole wide-open world was gettin' slammed shut. All because I'd gone to one more party. All because I'd gotten into the wrong car. All because I'd been too foolish to heed the warning shots that had been fired in my life so many times before that one stupid night.

The cop pulled me up on my feet and walked me over to his police car. Then he turned me around and got right up close to my face. He spoke real quiet, so no one else could hear him. He said, "I know who you are. I've seen you in the papers, and I know you have an opportunity to make it out of here, so I'm not going to ruin your chances by taking you to jail tonight."

He unlocked the handcuffs, and I rubbed my wrists where the metal had already rubbed me raw. "Just go home," he said, "and make sure you stay away from all this."

I nodded to him. I said, "Thank you." I looked him in the eye, hoping he could tell just how thankful I was. Then I turned and walked away as fast as I could without running.

I made it home safe that night only to face my dad. The cop who let me go tracked his number down and gave him a call before I got there, and I'll never forget the way he looked at me. He didn't lay a beating on me or anything like that. He just looked at me like I'd let him down, and that hurt. Both he and I knew just how close

I'd come to losing it all that night, and I swear his disappointment in me paled in comparison to my disappointment in myself.

"So, no more parties?" he said.

"No more parties," I responded.

I went to bed that night knowing it was only by the grace of God that I made it home at all. It was only by the grace of God that the shooter or one of those other kids who had their future on the line didn't say the gun was mine. It was only by the grace of God a cop didn't pull the trigger when I reached for my seat belt. It was only by the grace of God that the cop who let me go happened to recognize me from the paper. And that cop might as well have been an angel sent down from heaven, because the choice he made to let me go is the only reason I'm standing here today. Everything could have ended that night. Everything. And I knew it.

Did I pray about it? Did I start going to church again? Nah. I mostly thought I was lucky. I was still young and impulsive and thinking I was destined for bigger things all on my own. I was thankful, though. And I knew I was thankful to God.

# CHAPTER SIX

# SCRAMBLING

>> Remember that movie *Pleasantville*? Where a kid's whole world is black-and-white, but then something happens and his town suddenly turns to color?

That's what it was like for me moving on to the Penn State campus.

They call Penn State "Happy Valley," and I started to understand why the moment I arrived for training camp. Everywhere I went, people were in a good mood. They were helpful. They were friendly. Nobody looked at anybody with that hardened look people sometimes wore on their faces when they encountered strangers back in Wilmington. It seemed like absolutely everyone was smiling and laughing as they came and went from the dorms and buildings and locker rooms. I don't think I'd ever seen so many happy looking people.

Despite telling my dad I wouldn't go to any more parties back in Wilmington, I wound up going to a few "parties" almost as soon as I got to Penn State. It just seemed like the thing to do. Everyone was going. They invited me to come. How else was I going to make friends if I didn't go hang out with people? So I went.

Penn State parties weren't anything like parties back in my old neighborhood. They were more like social gatherings. It was just a bunch of people smiling and dancing and having a good time. Yeah they were drinking, and yeah some of them were smoking some weed, but it certainly didn't feel to me like a place where somebody might get shot, and I'm pretty sure no one else in the whole party looked over their shoulder or thought for one second about leaving early to avoid the let out.

I was still looking over my shoulder, though. For the first few weeks, I was still walking around with my guard up. That's just the way people walk around in a place like Wilmington when it's dark out or if they're in the wrong neighborhood.

Then one night I was on campus around two in the morning, walking past my dorm, and I spotted this white girl coming toward me all alone on the same path. I expected her to take one look at me—a big black dude in a hoodie—and turn around and go the other way or something. At the very least, I expected her to avert her eyes and walk past me all scared. But instead, she walked past me with a big smile on her face, as if we were on a crowded sidewalk full of people at two in the afternoon. She even said, "Hi."

I tipped my head and smiled a little bit to sort of say "hi" back, but I was speechless. I was like, *Wow. This is crazy. This really* is *Happy Valley.*

It suddenly hit me that if that girl felt safe, then I didn't have to watch behind my back on that campus either. I could do something that was previously unimaginable to me: I could just go out there and have fun. I could live my life without worrying that I might look at somebody the wrong way or bump their shoulder on the sidewalk and wind up on a T-shirt. The relief that gave me is hard to describe. And that led very quickly to me thinking, *Why would*

*I ever want to leave this place? Why would I ever want to go back to where I was?*

That was the moment I fell in love with Penn State, and honestly, it had been a bit of a struggle before that day. It was incredible to be there—to show up for summer workouts in June, and to walk into the beautiful locker room and training facility, and to start training with people who had more dedication to the sport than I'd ever encountered in my life. But it was *hard*.

First, there was the expectation to fit the mold of a certain appearance. I had worn braids before coming to Penn State, and when they were recruiting me, my linebacker coach had commented on my hair. "How'd you get your hair like that?" he asked me. I thought it was weird that he was asking about my hair, but then I realized that all the football players on the team had short hair. So in June, right before I went to school, I cut off my braids. That was my decision.

But as soon as I walked into the training facility, they made me go into the bathroom and shave off all my facial hair. During my campus visits, it had never occurred to me that no one on the football team had facial hair either. Not one of them. I'd been wearing facial hair for as long as I could grow it. It felt like I'd joined the army.

From that very first day, it felt like they wanted to break us.

Then there were the physical demands. We were training right along with the seniors who'd had four years of experience training at the college level, and we were expected to keep up with them from the start.

On day two they put us through ten 110-yard sprints, ten 80s, ten 60-yard shuttles. People were passing out! In the weight room they introduced us to the idea of a "negative," where you go all out on one of the machines and then when your body starts to give out, they make you keep going. Like, as soon as you're burned down, you gotta stand up and jog to the next machine and then do that machine, and the same thing with the next. I got so tired that I told our soon-to-be–star quarterback Daryll Clark, "I gotta use the bathroom." He didn't want to let me go at first, but I said, "I gotta go bad!" and the head trainer stepped in and said it was okay. So, I ducked into a bathroom stall and caught my breath for as long as I could. After a while, Daryll came in looking for me and started banging on the door. "Come on! It's time to get back to the weight room!" he said.

I lied and said, "I can't rush it!"

I eventually went back, and they worked me even harder. I got home that night and collapsed into bed like I was gonna die. I hurt so bad, I called my dad. "I don't know if I can do this," I said. "If this is gonna be my life for the next four years, I'm not sure if I really *want* football. I think I want to go home."

"Boy, be quiet," my dad said. "You ain't coming back home." He thought it was funny! I wasn't joking at all. But I could hear in the sound of his voice that as much as he was laughing at how hard they'd worked me, he was dead serious about not letting me quit.

When I went back the next day, it wasn't quite as bad. They still worked us hard, but it wasn't to the point of breaking like they'd laid on us the first two days. With each new day, I started to get more comfortable with the Penn State style of training, and I started doing really well. In fact, after two or three weeks, I started to love it. I went home exhausted at the end of every day and felt great about it. And soon enough, once we started actual practices, my coaches were giving me every indication that I had a shot at cracking the starting lineup. As a freshman! Seeing the possibility of that only made me want to work harder. And man, there's nothing like the feeling of working hard at something you love—knowing you're surrounded by the best of the best and that everybody there is trying to raise the bar along with you. There is nothing that comes *close* to that.

I was feeling so good that I decided to push the envelope a little bit.

For the three years after I broke my leg on the basketball court in high school, I'd worn a knee brace whenever I played. The doctor had recommended it as a temporary thing, but I went ahead and stuck with it for the rest of my high school career. Why risk a new injury, right? Plus, it just felt like part of my routine to pull that brace on before every practice and every game.

Once I got to college, I stopped wearing the brace, and I didn't have any problems. My leg felt good. But for some reason, at this one practice in August, I walked past my locker and I looked at that brace and contemplated putting it on. I just had a gut feeling that something wasn't right. I'm not sure why I had that sense, but I dismissed it. "No, just go out there and do what you do."

Toward the end of what turned out to be a particularly grueling practice, they sent me in for one last series of plays.

I occasionally found myself saying little prayers in my mind whenever I was called off the bench. "God, please watch over me and my teammates. I ask that you shower us with your blessings and keep us safe." That sort of thing. I'm not sure why I started doing that. And on this day, before I went in for that last play of the day, I distinctly remember praying, "God, please protect me as I go back in there for my last series."

Maybe I should have prayed a little harder. Maybe I should have prayed out loud. Maybe I should have taken a knee like those guys you see who are unashamed to show a little faith. Because on that play, during freshman training camp at the school I loved, the quarterback threw the ball to somebody down the sideline and I went chasing after him. I felt somebody grab my left shoulder from behind. I twisted—and I blew my knee out. It hurt, and it hurt bad. When the doctors surrounded me, I told them I was good and tried to get up and walk, but they stopped me and told me not to move until they checked my knee. One of the doctors started yanking my knee in different directions. It felt loose, like it was sliding in and out of place. That's when they told me I'd torn my ACL and MCL.

They had to carry me off the field.

I wound up on a table in the training room, crying, basically cursing God in my mind: *I prayed for you to protect me right before I went in for this play, and you didn't! If you loved me, you would have answered my prayer! There is no way that you love me, God!*

I didn't know much about ACLs then, but one of my older teammates kept telling me that people don't come back from that. "It's a career ender," he said. I don't think he had any ill intent when he said it, but it made me scared that my career might be over before it started.

At the very least, it's the sort of injury that leads to a season-long recovery, and that's exactly what the team doctor told me. I was done. They'd have to redshirt me for the season, which meant I could stay in school, get my education, and stay on scholarship without losing my chance to get back on the team as essentially a second-year freshman the following year. But for this year? There would be no football.

I was devastated.

Why didn't I listen to my gut and grab that brace? Talk about learning a lesson the hard way.

Even though I was newly injured, I still went to the team meeting after practice just to watch film with the rest of the guys. And while the whole defensive line was watching the film as that fateful moment replayed in front of our eyes, my defensive line coach took a water bottle and threw it across the room. He was devastated too.

Just like that, in the blink of an eye, my whole world changed. Again.

From that day forward, every morning, it would be my job to go to rehab and then hit the gym and work on training my upper body through weight lifting. And in the afternoons when the rest of the team went to practice, I'd be stuck on an exercise bike or training table. It felt like I was being punished. I could see the practice field.

I could see where I was supposed to be the whole time while I was stuck there on a bike going nowhere.

I was angry, and it took about a week for me to cool off. I had to force myself to remember that I'd made it through injuries before, and to believe that I could get through this one as well. I had to remind myself that whatever downtime I had would fly by if I kept my head on straight, and that it was entirely possible that I would come back better than ever. And once I did that, I apologized to God for overreacting. I prayed and promised Him, "I will never lose faith in you or blame you ever again, no matter what obstacles are put in my way."

Talking to God had become a fairly regular occurrence. He didn't answer me, of course. I didn't hear His voice or anything like my grandma used to talk about. Yet, there was something reassuring about those moments of prayer. I was grateful to God to be out of my old environment and at least *close* to living my dream. But looking back, I wish I'd done more of it. I wish I'd gone to church or found some other sort of support to get me through that time, because I got really down. I'd barely started to enjoy the freedom of living life in my own personal Pleasantville, and suddenly it went black-and-white on me again.

When you're young, it's hard to be patient. The rehab and weight lifting were just so boring. I found myself going to class and just staring out the window, wishing this injury would magically heal so I wouldn't have to wait until next year to play football. I didn't work as hard as I could have at my homework. I wasn't engaged or excited by any of it. I'd chosen to go in as a criminal justice major. I think it stemmed back to my short stint in jail in the fifth grade. The fingerprinting, the door slamming, not knowing what was gonna happen to me—I wanted to understand it all, how the whole system worked, thinking I might be able to go back and help kids like me keep their heads on straight. I loved the idea of using my degree to help people. But in the mood I was in currently, a lot of it just felt like work.

It was awkward sitting in some of those classrooms too. Howard High School was mostly black, and Penn State was mostly white. Sometimes I was the only black person and the only football player in the whole classroom.

In English class, our professor kept making us partner up, and every time she did it, nobody would partner up with me. I'm not sure if it was because I was black, or because I was a football player, or maybe it was because I felt so out of place that I just gave off an intimidating vibe. Maybe it was just me. Maybe I was acting out because of frustration, like I did when I was in fourth or fifth grade. But it felt so bad that I stopped going to class. I kept submitting my work and got all A's on the work itself. But after accumulating like ten absences, my academic advisor called me and my defensive line coach, Coach Johnson, in for a meeting.

I was clearly worn down.

"Man, you put me in a class where I'm the only black person!" I complained. Coach Johnson agreed that they shouldn't have put me in class by myself like that. At least being in class with another football player, regardless of race, might have made me feel less alone, he said. But it was too late to do anything about it that first semester. I had no choice but to suck it up.

I kept feeling sorry for myself, thinking, *What am I doing? I didn't come here to do this.*

Then the rehab training changed on me. Our staff got a new Russian STIM machine that was supposed to help your muscles learn how to fire so they could get stronger. It was like the machine they used in a scene from *Rocky IV* when Drago, the Russian fighter, was training for his fight. It hurt!

One morning I woke up and decided that I was done with that machine and I wasn't going to do it anymore. So, I walked into rehab acting like I wasn't feeling well, hoping they would give me a break. I lay down on a table that was three tables down from the machine and said I felt like I had to throw up and I didn't want to do the machine. Dusty, one of the student trainers, told me he didn't care—I was doing the machine anyway. He went and got the machine from the other table, brought it over to my table, and plugged it in. He then pulled the pads out to stick on my leg and my sickness act went out the window. I told him straight up, "If you put those pads on me, there's going to be a problem."

He walked away, and I started doing my other exercises. But I ended up getting into a heated argument with him twenty minutes later because I heard him talking about me with another student trainer. That got me called into another meeting with Coach Johnson, this time with the team's head trainer. Coach Johnson asked me what my problem was, and I told them: "They're killing me with the rehab and training. That Russian machine hurts, and I don't want to do it anymore. I don't even want to be here anymore. It's not worth it."

I was shocked when he turned to the head trainer and got angry that they were pushing me to the point I wanted to quit. When I saw that, I knew he had my back. I knew I had made the right choice coming to play for him.

• • •

During one of our breaks I went back to Wilmington for a visit, and a couple of my friends who were there, including my friend Charlie, convinced me to go to a party with them. They knew I'd sworn off parties after nearly getting arrested, but I think they were trying to cheer me up.

That's not what happened.

In the middle of the party my cell phone rang, and I stepped outside so I could hear. I was on the phone when something in my gut me told me I shouldn't be there. I should leave. *Now.*

This time I listened.

As I started to move toward the parking lot, someone else came out of the party and started walking behind me. Just as I got into my car, I noticed a black car pull out of a parking spot four spots away from mine.

The guy who came out behind me was standing by his car, which was parked right in front of mine. Suddenly someone stuck a revolver out of the window of the black car. I slammed the door shut and pulled the lever on my seat to recline it all the way back, as fast as I could. I hoped the metal doorframe would protect me. Shots rang out as if they were being fired all over, like someone wasn't aiming but randomly shooting.

Seconds later the shooting stopped. I heard the black car pull off and I sat up. Right in front of me I saw the guy who'd walked up after me laying on the ground. He was dead. All his friends came running out into the parking lot and started jumping up and down, crying and screaming. I spotted my friend Charlie sprinting through the lot, ducked real low in case any more bullets started flying, trying to hurry up and get to the car, and I thought, *That could have been Charlie just now. That could have been* me.

Seeing somebody get killed right in front of me, looking at that dead body just a couple of feet away from me, didn't make me feel sick. It didn't freak me out. I felt bad for the kid and his friends, of course, but I'd been in that environment for so long that coming that close to it wasn't an unexpected thing. In fact, I fully expected it—and I knew that wasn't how I wanted to feel anymore.

In that moment I told myself that whatever I had to go through at Penn State, I was gonna go through it. Whatever pain I had to suffer in order to get over my injury was far less than the pain I would suffer if I came back to Wilmington and raised a family in this environment, knowing that every day either me or one of my kids could be that kid there, dead on the ground. I refused to let that happen. Seeing that boy get shot right in front of me was the instant I stopped giving myself the choice to quit school and come home. In my mind, in my heart—once and for all—that choice no longer existed.

The only way forward was forward.

I'm not sure why it took so many warning shots for me to fully grasp the message. Actually, I think there were still parts of the message I didn't get. I left that party thinking it wasn't necessarily going to parties that was the bad thing; it was just going to parties in the wrong places, in the wrong environments.

I wasn't meant for this life. I wasn't meant to "live fast and die young," that mentality that so many city kids seem to idolize. Nah. I was meant for something else. I needed to get out, and to get out for good. I made up my mind that whatever I had to overcome in order to make that happen, I would overcome. Period.

It's funny, but when you say you're going to do something, when you say you want something, life has a way of testing just how bad you want it. I mean, truly, when I made up my mind to overcome whatever I had to overcome, I had no idea just how much I would have to overcome!

As my ACL healed and I finished out my freshman year, I thought the overcoming was nearing an end. I thought I'd gotten through the worst of it, and the rest of my time at Penn State would be easier because of it. That wasn't the case. It turns out I was still at the very beginning of learning the hard way.

The week after I was injured, after I basically cursed God for letting me get hurt, I had prayed and told God I would never react that way again, no matter what obstacles are thrown in my way. That promise was put to the test, because after a whole year of rehabilitation, after working my butt off to get back to a point where I could run and jump and play football again, I made it to training camp—and almost immediately got injured again. This time we were having a scrimmage at Beaver Stadium. I was playing one of my blocks and holding one of the men up in front of me, and somebody got thrown into the pile and hit my leg. I felt a snap in my lower leg, down by my ankle. I fell to the ground. I took off my helmet and threw it across the field in frustration. I lay on the ground in disbelief. It was like the same scene from before with the doctors surrounding me. The pain started to intensify and I started hyperventilating. The team doctor tried to calm me down by asking me to say my ABCs, but I couldn't make it past E.

They rushed me to the hospital and discovered that my fibula was broken, way down low. They had to put a plate and ten screws in just to put it back together.

Once again, they told me that I would be out of commission for the entire season.

Once again, I felt angry. I felt enraged!

Only this time, I didn't curse God. I held back that instinct to blame it on God or to see this injury as something I should feel sorry about. I tried to control my emotions and recognize this injury and this surgery and what I knew would be a long recovery for what it was: another test, another obstacle, from which I would continue learning through patience and persistence to overcome. I had overcome my broken leg in high school, and look where it led me. It led me to Penn State! So to overcome not one but two season-ending-type injuries back-to-back, where was *this* gonna lead me?

Instead of focusing on the negative, I did my best to focus on the fact that I was grateful to be where I was. After all I'd seen in Wilmington, I was grateful just to be alive! It felt good to have this place, this time, this chance. I was learning patience and persistence and finding peace through prayer. And because of what I'd learned already, I did my best to focus on the possibility that this just might be the greatest thing that ever happened to me.

I know that sounds like a big leap of faith, but that was the leap I needed to make in order to get through it—because I wound up crying almost every day and asking again and again, "Why me?" I was facing my second year of not playing, of not getting to where I wanted to go, of being *at Penn State* and forced to stay on the sidelines. If I didn't focus on the potential positive my injury might bring, I don't think I could have survived.

I was also grateful that I had the support of my parents. Even in college, when I wound up in the hospital, my parents showed up. My mom took time off of work to show up and stay right there at the hospital with me every single day, right up until I was released.

Having that kind of support definitely helped me keep my head on straight.

It wasn't easy, though. Staying focused never is, and I definitely slipped up a few times. I did my best to get back to focusing on the road ahead. I kept thinking about the very real possibility that playing well at Penn State could lead me to the NFL. I tried to put my head down and get back to the grind.

I was still young, though. Patience was still a problem.

Halfway through the year—pedaling that stationary bike with my hands again while my teammates were out on the field for the hundredth time, and struggling to get around a snowy campus on a blue electric scooter because I wasn't supposed to step on that leg—my whole mentality started to slide downhill. I saw my teammates progressing in ways that I couldn't, because I wasn't out there holding the football. I felt like I was two years behind everyone I'd started out with. I began to slip into thoughts of, *What am I doing? Why am I here?* And it wasn't long before I started to act on those thoughts.

I started finding excuses to skip my practice-time workouts. It got so bad that I'd pretend to fall asleep studying on the couch in the player lounge just so I'd miss my bus to the stadium. On days when I went, I gave minimal effort and then went back to my apartment and went to bed. I'm not sure if I was clinically depressed. I was never diagnosed or anything, but my body started to feel like I felt in my mind. Like it didn't want to move. Like it wanted to give up. I tried to pick myself up by going to the stadium for our home games, just to feel that energy. But I couldn't travel for away games, so I sat and watched them from my campus apartment—watching the TV flicker over the toe of the plastic boot that surrounded my ankle and lower leg.

In my mind, I had removed the option of ever going home. I refused to let that happen. But it seemed like that promise I made wasn't enough to keep me from giving up in a different sort of way.

The fact that our team had a really good season that year only added to my frustration. We were undefeated at midseason when we faced Ohio State, Penn State's biggest rival. I wanted with everything in me to be a part of that game, and once again I sat around feeling sorry for myself, complaining that I wasn't there. I watched on TV from my apartment as they played that night game in the Horseshoe, Ohio State's massive stadium in Columbus. It was just so frustrating to be stuck at home when I knew I was supposed to be under those lights.

The game was incredible. It was a brawl, back and forth and back and forth all night. By the tail end of fourth quarter, we were down, and Ohio had the ball. It seemed like our chances of staging a comeback were slipping away every second. Then something amazing happened. The Buckeyes tried to run a quarterback sneak to get to first down, but instead of going straight up the line, their quarterback decided to try to bounce it outside. Our safety came up and hit him, and the ball flew out of his hands. Then our linebacker, NaVorro Bowman, recovered the fumble. We marched it down the field and scored! We won the game 13–6! Suddenly the sound on my TV was overwhelmed by the sound of Penn State students all around me, pouring out of the apartment building and toward downtown as the whole campus broke into a celebration.

I got on my scooter and headed downtown with the crowd. It was a sight I had never seen before. It was like every student at Penn State was on College Avenue having one big party celebrating the win.

When I got back to my apartment, I started crying because I wanted to be a part of the reason they were celebrating.

That's when something snapped, and it wasn't a bone this time. Something in my mind snapped. What was I doing sitting around feeling sorry for myself? I was at Penn State! This was *my* school. That was *my* team that just won that game. That was *my* cheering squad out there running all over downtown right now. I had a whole campus that would get behind me if I would just get back in the game.

Over the course of the next week, I stopped saying, "Why me?" and started saying, "Why *not* me? When I get my opportunity, when I step back on the field after this, I'm gonna make things happen. I'm gonna make my mark. I'm gonna leave my legacy!" So what if my other teammates were out there living their dreams? I stopped using the jealousy I had toward them to complain about my situation and decided to use it to push me to go out there and get the things I was jealous *of*, plus more.

I went back to the gym. While my leg healed, I got the rest of myself into the best shape of my life. And when the leg was ready to come out of its plastic shell, I gave every single rehab exercise my full attention and focus until I beat the odds—and I beat the prognosis. I didn't miss the whole season. The doctors said I could get back on the field right before our final game of the year. The hard work I put in paid off.

Now I had a choice to make. Our last game was against Michigan State. Because I'd been injured in two back-to-back seasons, I could have applied for a grey-shirt—a status that would have allowed me to add another year to my college career, to give me a chance to make up for all that lost time. That would basically allow me some leeway, like, if it took me a while to fully get back up to speed after this injury, I'd have a whole other year to prove to the NFL that I was a player they ought to be interested in drafting.

But in order to do that, I would have to sit out of that final game. If I played at all, for even one play, any possibility of a grey-shirt year was gone.

To me, the choice was easy. I'd worked two full years to get back on the football field to finally get a chance to play my first game for Penn State. There was no *way* I was giving up my chance to go play.

"Are you sure?" my line coach asked me. "Because if you need that extra year to get yourself right to go to the NFL, you're basically giving that up."

"Yeah. I'm sure," I said. "Put me in the game."

So, he put me in the game—and it sucked. I just wasn't ready. For all the muscle work I'd done and rehabilitation I'd done, I hadn't had enough time on the practice field to get back in the shape I needed to be in to play at that level. I was tired after the first play. I was dead tired after three. Six plays in I was breathing so hard you'd have thought I'd just climbed Mt. Everest without an oxygen tank. Finally, as if to drive it all home, on the seventh play I went and hit a spin move, and the offensive tackle came and nearly knocked my head off.

Seven plays and the game was over.

I thought, *Did I really just erase my grey-shirt year for this?*

Don't get me wrong, though: I thought that with a great big smile on my face. I didn't care that it hurt. I didn't care that I was tired. I didn't care that I only got in the game for seven plays. I looked around at that stadium full of people and listened as they roared on every play. I heard those cheers, and I fully appreciated that I was *there*. I now knew what it felt like play football at a Division 1 school after two years of nothing but anticipation.

If those seven plays were all I got, *ever*, I think it would have been worth it.

Plus, I knew that wasn't the case. I knew I was just getting started.

I knew in my heart that good things were coming—because I had overcome.

# CHAPTER SEVEN

# SECOND HALF

≫ As I prepared to go into my junior year, I was feeling good. No obstacles. No injuries. Nothing to overcome—or so I thought. I was ready to play. And I did.

One weekend, rapper Wiz Khalifa came to Penn State for a concert. And for those who don't know, when Wiz Khalifa comes to town, you can bet that anybody who's going to show up for that concert is going to show up high. Everyone I knew was going. I knew it was wrong. I knew I shouldn't be smoking as an athlete. But I was in a place where we were playing hard and living life and having fun. I probably felt a little invincible at this point, so I threw caution to the wind and joined my friends. When I went to the football building the next day for my workout, somebody approached me and said, "Mr. Still, we have you on our list. You're getting drug tested today."

My heart dropped. I knew there was no way I was going to pass that test.

When the results came back, they called me into the office.

"Devon," they said, "you just failed the drug test for marijuana. If you fail again we will have no choice but to release you from the team and kick you out of school."

No sooner did I get back to my dorm room than my phone rang. It was my dad. "I just found out that you failed your drug test," he said. (Apparently they informed parents of these things.) "Now, I can't tell you what to do because you're a grown man. You're in college now. But, what I want to tell you is you're about to blow the opportunity of a lifetime. You have a chance to live a life that most people only dream about, and you're about to blow it for what? Having fun? Smoking weed? You have the chance to change the whole demographics of your family, and you're willing to risk all that just to have fun with your friends?"

I couldn't believe I'd been so stupid. So careless. I felt like a failure. Like I was letting my family down and my city down because there weren't a lot of people that made it out, and I had a chance to show what's possible.

I promised my dad then and there that I wouldn't pick up weed again. I know I was still young, and young people don't always make the right decisions. But I couldn't understand why I'd done it. Why had I lost my focus? Why had I treated all of this opportunity I had in front of me with such a careless attitude? I wouldn't really understand it until years later, but what I think now is that I was just being selfish. If I'd have stopped and thought about the sacrifices my parents made to get me where I was, if I'd have stopped and thought about the sacrifices my coaches and teachers had made, too, and the time and effort they'd put into helping me live out my dream of playing football, would I have been so careless? How could I have lived with myself if I'd have gotten kicked out of school and let all of those people down? Not to mention myself.

It wasn't the only questionable decision I made that year.

I had been dating that girl from my senior year of high school off and on while I was at Penn State. I hadn't seen her in a while, so she decided to come up to celebrate my birthday with me. One thing led to another, and over the course of the next few months we found out she was pregnant.

I wasn't thinking about what I'd learned in church about the sanctity of marriage or the sacred bond between a man and a woman. Maybe I wasn't thinking at all. Maybe I was just being young and impulsive. But the idea of having a child while I was still young and on the way up in life didn't seem scary to me. Maybe it should have, but it didn't.

Sure, I was worried about the added responsibilities. Every once in a while I'd panic about it and shed a tear on the way to practice, wondering how I was going to afford to support a baby. I didn't have a job outside of school, and the only extra money that came in was through Pell Grants. Other football players my age were using their Pell Grants to buy electronics and have a little fun money while the rest of their room-and-board costs were paid by scholarships or their parents' money. I couldn't do that. So sure, I was nervous. But more than that, once the shock of it all settled down, I was actually excited at the thought of bringing a child into the world just because of where I now lived. The thought of my kid being born in a place where he or she wouldn't have to look over his or her shoulder all the time made me smile. I got excited and proud just thinking about being able to give that kind of life to my child from the start.

So I started looking at off-campus apartments that could fit all three of us on my meager budget.

In the background of all of this, though, another tragedy was on my mind. During the prior school year, two of my old high school friends, both talented athletes back in Wilmington, were leaving a flag football game one day when another driver T-boned their car. One of them, my friend who we all called "Money," was thrown out the back window and injured so badly he would never play football again. He wound up in a coma for over a month. The other, my buddy John, actually died. He was gone for a couple of minutes until the paramedics miraculously revived him, and then he was in a coma for over a month too.

It seemed like near misses and flat-out tragedies were following all of us Howard High football players around like some kind of curse. I didn't think it would affect me at Penn State. I thought I was safe. I thought I was out. I thought I'd escaped. So I tried to stay focused on the blessings I had, but I worried all the time about what might happen next to another member of my crew.

John made a pretty miraculous recovery. He wound up playing well enough to get back into football at Delaware State later that year. But I could tell he wasn't the same. Like I said, John was one of the quickest people I've ever seen play the sport of football. Nobody could tackle him. He should have been on track to make it to the NFL. I prayed that he'd make a full recovery and get back in top shape.

I prayed for my own protection as well, and this time God seemed to be smiling in my direction. I felt like I had successfully passed my test or something. Training camp that summer went off without a hitch. No injuries. In fact, everything started to click for me that year, just like it did in my junior year of high school. But this wasn't high school anymore. This was Division 1 football, and I was finally playing without injury.

Knowing I had a baby on the way served as some extra motivation to play my best. I wanted to secure my future. I wanted to make my mark, more than ever. And thanks to God, I did. JoePa and my defensive line coach played me in every single game. When we played Michigan that year, I sacked Tate Forcier. It was my first college sack, and it was a big one: a 10-yard loss to help lift us to a 35–10 win. I had three tackles each against Syracuse and our big rival, Ohio State, too. Over the course of that single season I made nineteen tackles.

Altogether, I was on the field for 348 plays that year. My tiny, one-game, seven-play debut seemed like a distant memory. And I knew I was still growing. I still had improving to do. In my mind I still had a long way to go, and that was a good feeling. I was up for the challenge. I could see the NFL waiting at the end of this road I was on. I could see the possibility of huge dreams coming true.

And in the background of all of that was the realization that I was about to become a father.

• • •

On May 6, 2010, I stood in the delivery room taking video as Leah came into the world. My mom was right there, too, helping with the birthing process and everything.

I stayed up that whole night in the hospital. I stared at her in her little crib, like, I just couldn't believe I had a child. Then I wound up laying down in my own hospital bed in the room with Leah on my chest the whole time, holding her and staring at her. If somebody came into that room not knowing any better, they might have thought I was the one who gave birth to her! I couldn't let her go. I didn't want to be without her for even one second. I'd never felt a love like that.

Looking at that child, I knew somewhere deep down in my soul that I needed to be the best father I could be. I wanted to give her the best life I could give her. And I knew that a great big part of achieving that meant I had to be the best football player I could be—for *her*. It was about Leah. Everything I'd worked for, everything I'd achieved, I realized it had *all* been for her. It *all* had a bigger purpose. My whole reason for being suddenly felt bigger than the small, selfish way I'd been thinking about my purpose here on this earth.

Maybe that sort of deep thinking doesn't engulf everybody who has a baby, but it most definitely engulfed me that night—and has continued to do so pretty much every day since.

Holding that tiny baby girl in my arms, I felt more motivation to achieve greatness in my life than I ever knew I had in me—all because it wasn't about me. It was about *her*. It dawned on me that the motivational idea of "giving your all" was actually about *giving*. I needed to do my best in order give the best of me to my daughter. I needed to do my best in order to *give* my daughter the life she deserved.

Who could have predicted that having a daughter would turn out to be the greatest blessing and the greatest motivator I'd ever encountered?

Leah's arrival was the inspiration that got me to stop going to parties. Cold turkey. I just stopped showing up. Friends kept asking where I was all the time, and I told 'em, "Nowhere. I was just at home with my baby girl."

My desire to drink or smoke or lose focus in any other way went out the window.

Nothing else interested me except focusing on football and going home to my daughter.

I managed to find the three of us a low-income house a few miles from campus. It was a townhome with two stories and plenty of room for everything we needed. The only issue was distance. Leah's mom had a car, but I'd grown used to being close to everything on campus, where there were shuttle buses to help students get around. Now? I needed a vehicle for myself, and I couldn't afford a car.

So I took some of my Pell Grant money and I bought myself a scooter. A bright-yellow scooter that was the ugliest thing I'd ever seen. But it worked. It got me where I needed to go. Me, a six foot five inch football player riding that bright-yellow scooter all over campus. I got so much grief about the color that I went and painted it matte black before summer was over. But there was nothing I could do about the size of it. It looked like a minibike under my body. And there was nothing I could do about the fact that it was the only vehicle I had when the weather turned colder. I would ride that scooter back and forth to school even in the middle of 6 a.m.

central Pennsylvania snowstorms. I'd bundle up in layers, sometimes wearing two coats on top of each other just trying to stay warm on that ride, and my face just about froze off.

It wasn't easy juggling fatherhood with my academic schedule and football, but compared to the effort I had to put in to recover from injuries and surgeries, these new struggles seemed like nothing. I wasn't going home each night to a lonely dorm room to wallow in self-pity. I was going home to a townhouse where I got to spend time with my new baby in her princess-themed room.

Things weren't perfect, though. Leah's mom and I didn't really agree on much. We seemed to have a hard time getting along after Leah was born. She picked up a job once Leah was old enough to be left at daycare, but she didn't have any family or other support around at Penn State. I was gone a lot because of all my school and football obligations, so it was tough on her.

It was tough on me too. There were days Leah's mom had to work and I had no choice but to bring Leah with me to team meetings.

The coaching staff, including Coach Johnson, were real supportive. They never hesitated when I said I might need to bring her. "Sure," they said. "Whatever you have to do."

It was weird, sitting with a crew of six-foot-plus linemen, watching tape, talking strategy, then suddenly hearing my baby girl's voice start crying for some milk. I'd cuddle her and give her a bottle and quiet her down as gently as I could, but sometimes I'd have to step out of the room, and I'd worry that I was missing out on something I should be listening to. I never missed much, though. It all worked out. It was great having Leah with me on campus. Everybody loved seeing her and showed her all kinds of affection. You don't see a lot of babies on a college campus, so just the sight of her spread smiles wherever we went.

All in all, the three of us were leading a pretty good life. We were safe. We were comfortable. We had a nice roof over our heads. And as I headed into my senior year, inspired by Leah, I started playing with more focus than I'd ever played with in my life. The accumulation of upper-body strength I'd developed in my first two years at Penn State combined with Coach Johnson's hard-core training style had me in what I thought was the best shape of my life. The results showed up in my stats. I started in twelve games, delivering thirty-nine tackles and one pass breakup over the course of the season. That included ten tackles for loss and four sacks. Three of my tackles and a sack were in one game, against number one Alabama. In our win over Minnesota, I sacked Adam Weber in the end zone for my first career safety. I made a career-high six tackles in *one game* against Michigan. I made four tackles and one sack for a six-yard loss in our 35–21 comeback victory over Northwestern too. In total I was on the field for 710 snaps—nearly double my junior-year showing. But I still had a ways to go. I knew I could do even better with one more season.

The more impressive stat to me, though, was how fast little Leah was growing. By Christmastime she was sitting up in her bouncy seat and kicking her legs to whatever music we put on.

"Ooooh, she's gonna be a dancer!" my mom said.

I didn't want to play her the kind of music I'd grown up on, so I bought her some Kidz Bop CDs, and she lit up every time we put 'em on. I could hardly stand listening to those cheesy, kid-friendly pop songs, but she giggled and smiled so much whenever she heard them, I couldn't help but play them for her all the time.

I swear my little girl lit up every time I walked in the room, too, and I don't think there is any finer feeling a father can feel than seeing his little girl smile at him. If I had a rough day at practice or a long trip back from a losing game, she'd flash that smile and every care I had went out the window. I'd sit on the floor and make funny faces, and she'd laugh and giggle, and that would make me laugh, which made her laugh even more. I started capturing these moments on my phone, and I swear Leah knew what a camera was even at seven months old. She lit up every time I turned my phone on and then laughed at the sight of herself when I played back those videos.

She seemed to like anything pink, including her favorite little headbands. And both her grandmothers bought her onesies that said "Daddy's Little Girl" and outfits that looked like little cheerleader costumes. It felt like she was my biggest fan, and there's no doubt I was hers. She loved all kinds of girlie toys and stuffed animals right from the start, so I couldn't help but pick some up for her whenever I traveled for games, even though we were broke most of the time.

Honestly, I thought my heart was gonna melt the first time she said "Da-da." It wasn't quite "Daddy" yet. She was just imitating sounds, like, "da da da da" and "ma ma ma ma." But it was the coolest sound in the world.

She was growing up so fast that I felt an urgency to step it up. Like I needed to take more responsibility for my life. I wanted to put myself on a fast track to becoming not just a football player, but a leader—the type of guy who gets noticed by the NFL for more than just his stats.

There was another reason I felt that new sense of urgency.

During that school year, something happened to my best friend, Charlie. He was out with some friends one night, celebrating a great practice he'd had in front of some NFL scouts. He was walking along the edge of a sidewalk when a driver swerved too close to the curb and plowed right into him. The accident messed up his legs so bad, he wasn't able to play football anymore. His career was over. Just like that.

We got into this really deep talk one night after that. "Something's wrong, man. Everyone we know is dying. Everyone's gettin' hurt. Something's not right," he said.

Once again, we wondered if there was some kind of a curse following our old teammates around.

Charlie decided that maybe it had something to do with the kind of life we'd all been living. So he decided to make a change. He was already an occasional churchgoer. His mom was a dedicated member of an Evangelical church. But he decided to go deeper into his faith. He started going to church regularly.

It kind of blew my mind he could go through such a powerful transformation so quickly. I didn't understand it. I wasn't going to church. I wasn't doing anything more than saying the occasional prayer. I didn't see a spiritual transformation as something I wanted or needed. I thought I was safe from any "curse" because I had made it out to Penn State, so it just never crossed my mind.

Still, it added to my desire to step up in life. It made me realize how quickly things can change.

I had stayed in the background most of that football season. I played solid, but I never stepped into any sort of a leadership role at all. I was quiet, just like I'd stayed quiet during the whole recruiting process out of high school, and during the three years since. But when we made it to the Outback Bowl against Florida on New Year's Day 2011, I started to get fired up in a whole new way. Knowing our team captains were graduating at the end of that year, I saw an opportunity for me to take a shot at stepping into their shoes before the start of that game. I can't explain what made me do it, but right before we went out to play that game I called the whole team into a huddle. I hadn't prepared a speech. I didn't even know what I was doing. I just looked around at my teammates and opened my mouth and a speech came out. It's like two years of not being able to touch a football followed by two years of quietly giving it my all combined with wanting to build a better life for Leah all came rolling out of my heart.

"It's time for us to step up. It's time to go out there and play the best game we have, and leave *everything* on the field," I said.

A couple of my teammates responded, "Yeah."

"This is our chance to show the country what they're going to have to deal with next season. Give it everything you got so they will make no mistakes about who we are!"

I kept talking, and more teammates responded. I found a rhythm, and the responses got louder. I could see and feel my team start to get pumped up. I wish I had a recording or could remember everything I said that day, but every word was spontaneous. Every word came straight from my heart. I know I wrapped up by saying something along the lines of, "We need to play for each other—and if anyone gets in our way, if they're not wearing blue and white, then they're gettin' hit!"

The whole team roared at those words. I think I shocked them. The eyes of the coaches and team doctors and everybody around us were fixed on mine, hanging on every word. Like, no one saw that coming. Not even *me*. My words got everyone so fired up that we went out there and played our hearts out. I personally played my best game ever, with a career-high seven tackles—six of them solo—and a 3.5-yard tackle for loss.

That New Year's Day was a game changer for me. Not only did it set me up for an honorable mention in the All–Big Ten selection that year, but it changed the way my teammates and my coaches saw me. In one moment, with one speech, my team now saw me as not just a player, but as a leader.

My teammates didn't forget it, either. When it came time to choose new captains for the 2011 season—my fifth-year senior year—they chose me in a unanimous decision.

My thoughts and dreams of stepping up and taking on a bigger role in my own life in the hopes of doing better for my daughter were already coming true.

• • •

The teamwork I was building on the field was a whole lot better than the teamwork I was building at home.

Leah's mom and I weren't getting along. The plain fact of the matter is we had a child when we were too young to handle it. That caused a lot of tension, and we knew that wasn't healthy for Leah. So we decided things needed to change.

My future depended on me staying in school, and the future I wanted for Leah depended on me making my NFL dreams come true. But there was no way I could care for Leah by myself while going to school full time and playing football, which meant I really didn't have a choice in what happened next.

It was one of the hardest decisions I've ever had to make, but Leah needed to stay with her mom—and her mom decided to move to North Carolina, where Leah's maternal grandmother would be there to help out while Leah's mom went back to school.

The idea of saying goodbye to my daughter for potentially months at a time was devastating to me. But I knew the pain of watching her grow up in a toxic environment was worse.

Before I knew it, just before we celebrated Leah's first birthday, the day came to say goodbye. Leah was all tucked in a blanket in her car carrier, her little stocking feet sticking out over the end of it. She'd grown so much. I kissed her on the forehead and told her I'd see her real soon, and she smiled up at me. She grabbed my pinky with her tiny hand and squeezed.

"Oh, that's a good grip," I said.

I put my hands over my eyes, and Leah put her hands over hers, and we played a little peek-a-boo, which had become a new thing for us lately. I said "Boo!" and she laughed and laughed.

Next thing I knew they were in the car. I watched them drive away.

Just like that my whole world changed. Again. My new reason for everything, my inspiration, my baby girl who filled up my heart every day, was gone.

# CHAPTER EIGHT

# SAFETY

>> If it weren't for my cheering squad, my teammates and class-mates at Penn State, I don't think I would've made it through that change. I was used to seeing my daughter every day. Now, I'd be lucky to see her on breaks. I'd have to come up with money to fly to North Carolina or to fly them up to me. I didn't know how that was going to be possible.

Thankfully I had a support team. I had people who cared about me. I had teammates, plus a campus and a community that I was a part of, who were willing to take me in.

I started socializing again, and I'll never forget the looks I got when I showed up at some small parties after a whole year away. People acted like they were seeing a ghost or something. But they embraced that ghost with love and laughter.

Skype was getting more popular and easy to use by that time, so I could see Leah sometimes and know that at least my baby girl wouldn't forget what I looked and sounded like. But it didn't take long for me to realize that the only way this situation was going to truly get better was for *me* to get better. It was on me, once again, to step up my game, to make my career into everything I ever dreamed it could be. To go into my very last season of college football with my sights set high. To become an All-American, to earn the respect of coaches and players not just at my school, but all over the conference and across the country. To gain the attention of NFL scouts and make my way toward earning a top spot in the 2012 Draft. If I could do all of that, I wouldn't have to worry about money anymore. I wouldn't have to worry about anything, I thought. I could do whatever it took to make sure Leah was in my life.

Not having to worry about taking care of a baby at home that season definitely gave me the room I needed to focus on accomplishing what I needed to accomplish.

As I headed to training camp that summer—my last summer before my last semester at Penn State—I got talking about my ambitions to defensive line coach Elijah Robinson (who would later go on to coach at Texas A&M). He probably doesn't even remember saying this to me, but the advice he gave me changed my life. He said, "Devon, if you want to become an All-American, you have to start training like an All-American right now. You have to practice like an All-American, right now!"

Nobody becomes an All-American by chance. It's not just about somebody's size or talent. It's about putting in the hard work—harder than anybody else is willing to work. I don't know why I didn't think like that all on my own before that moment, but that moment was when I started training like an All-American. I got up before everybody else to go work out. Not just some days, but every day. I stayed longer in the weight room than everybody else, not just some days, but every day. I needed to gain an advantage over my peers who'd started before me, who had two full years to get ahead of me while I was sidelined with injuries. That meant I had a lot of making up to do. So I got back to training with the skill players, running routes with them just like I did with my friends in high school.

I didn't waste time feeling sorry for myself for having to make up all that lost time. I was excited just thinking about being an All-American. I was excited thinking about getting drafted by the NFL. I swear I could hear the announcer calling my name out. I could picture myself walking across the stage at the Draft in front of a great big audience with millions of people watching on TV.

I thought I was in the best shape of my life during my 2010 season. But I wasn't even close. By the time we played the first game of my fifth-year senior year in the fall of 2011, I'd reached a whole other level. I played better than I'd ever played, consistently, in *every* game. I stood up as team captain and used my voice to inspire my teammates, while simultaneously hoping my dedication to training served as a silent example of leadership as well. And I know that my efforts played at least some small role in the fact that we just kept winning.

We were 7–1 overall, and 4–0 in the Big Ten, as we headed into one of the most monumental games I could imagine: if we could win against Illinois that October 29, we would be handing our coach, Joe Paterno, his 409th victory. That win would make JoePa the winningest coach in Division 1 history.

The conditions that day were anything but ideal. It was freezing cold, with a slushy mix of rain and snow falling over the field, not to mention falling all over that stadium full of 106,000 fans who showed up collectively hoping and praying to witness history.

The weather wasn't the only thing that was sloppy, though. So was our performance. We fumbled the ball six times and lost possession on two of those, but we somehow kept scrambling back and keeping the Illinois Illinis from scoring—until the third quarter, when they scored a touchdown. From there we went back and forth with nothing but a field goal on the boards despite some really good plays, including one where I sacked their quarterback.

Late in the fourth quarter, my defensive line stopped Illinois short on a hard drive, giving us one last chance to make something happen. We had possession at our 20-yard line with the clock tick-ing down. As I walked to the bench, I noticed a bunch of the younger guys and even some of the other defensive players sitting there talk-ing and joking around, barely paying attention to the game.

JoePa wasn't down on the field with us. He'd been injured in an accidental preseason hit when one of our receivers plowed into him on the sidelines. That tough old man stood up and kept coaching the whole practice until the doctors made him get in the golf cart and get X-rays. I don't know where that man got his toughness. His hip was still giving him a lot of trouble weeks later, though, so he was up watching in the booth under doctor's orders. I knew for a fact that nobody on the team would've sat there silent and not paying attention if Joe Paterno was standing in front of them. So, I decided to take on the role of the motivator he was. I mean, he could motivate people just by standing there. That's what kind of respect he commanded. But I had to yell.

"Get up! Up, up, up!" I shouted, running up and down the side-line waving my arms. "Get up on that sideline and cheer on our offense!"

Sure enough, once our whole team was rallying together and cheering for each other, our offense sprung to life. Quarterback Matt McGloin took us from our 20 to the Illini 32 on three long completions. Then he shot a beautiful pass to our wide receiver Derek Moye in the end zone—only the play was broken up by Illinois corner Justin Green. Green got whistled for pass interfer-ence, and that gave us a second chance. I kept rallying our guys on the sidelines, and the crowd got as pumped as we were. Four plays later our running back, Silas Redd, forced his way through the Illinois defensive line into the end zone for a touchdown—with just 1:08 left in the game.

The whole stadium erupted in cheers. We made the extra point. The cheers got even louder. The scoreboard lit up: 10–7. Every one of us knew what this would mean to Joe Paterno if we could just hold on. The Illinois offense started the next possession at their own 17, and they fought like crazy. They pushed and pushed, almost as if they were feeding on our massive home-crowd energy and using it for themselves. We had a hard time holding them back. I was frustrated, as was the rest of my line, but with seconds to go, we managed to hold them at our 25-yard line. The clock was down to a couple of seconds. They had no choice but to go for a do-or-die field goal attempt from 42 yards out in that terrible weather.

We'd done our job. Now, all we could do was watch.

The fans didn't just sit there and watch, though. They did something I've never seen before in college football. The whole student section ran together behind the goal post, waving, yelling, doing everything they could to distract the kicker. It was wild! Illinois's Derek Dimke kicked that ball as the clock ticked down to "2" and then "1" as it soared through the air, and the clock hit "0" as it bounced off the right-hand upright.

"Let's go!" I shouted, jumping up into the air as our whole team ran onto the field, celebrating as one, knowing we had just lifted our legendary coach to an entirely new, seemingly unbreakable spot in the record books of college football history. The noise was deafening! I wouldn't be surprised if the shouts coming from that stadium could be heard all the way back in Wilmington.

When Joe finally made it down to the field to join in the celebration, he stopped and looked at me with tears of joy in his eyes.

"Thank you," he said. "Thank you for rallying the sideline when I couldn't be down here."

At that moment, Joe Paterno had reached the very height of his coaching career. The apex. I can't even express how amazing it felt to have played my part in making it happen for him. And here he was, thanking *me*.

Hard work can sometimes bring rewards you don't see coming. Training like an All-American, stepping up and becoming a leader—all of that led me to that moment, when one of the greatest coaches ever stopped and thanked me for my role, even though all I wanted to do was thank *him*. He was the one who'd shown up in person to convince me to come to Penn State. He was the one who'd established a program full of jaw-dropping discipline that made me want to pay that kind of attention to detail in every part of my life. He was the one who'd led such an awe-inspiring career. He was the one who'd inspired me to want to lead, both in words and by example; to step up and earn the respect of my team and everyone else.

I owed a lot to that man, and it just put the biggest smile on my face knowing that all of us had worked together to bring him that achievement.

When my head hit the pillow that night, I was still smiling. With the sound of that 106,000-strong crowd still ringing in my ears, all I could think was, "How far can we take this? How far can we go for Joe? Let's take him to win number 410, 411, 412. . . ."

• • •

Eight days later, all the smiles went away.

Our coaches called a squad meeting and told us "some news" was gonna come out. They didn't tell us what that news was, but they did say it might shake things up a bit. They told us not to talk to any media if people called us, but all in all they didn't make it seem like it was going to be that big a deal. I walked out of there thinking, *Penn State's a prestigious school. How bad could any news be?*

I had no idea.

That night I was home watching TV when the news they were talking about finally broke: Jerry Sandusky, a former Penn State assistant coach, in fact a former secondary coach who had worked under Joe Paterno from the late 1960s until 1999, was arrested on forty counts of child sexual assault.

"What?" I yelled right out loud.

The news said some of the alleged incidents happened under Joe's watch at Penn State, in the locker room and showers at the Lasch Building where me and the rest of the team worked out every day.

I'd *met* Jerry Sandusky. I'd seen him around. He'd been retired for years, but he still hung out in the weight room sometimes. I thought he was a quirky, weird kind of guy, but he never really said a whole lot, so I never paid him much attention. But the things they were saying this man had done—it made me sick to my stomach. He'd founded a charity back in the 1970s aimed at helping under-privileged and at-risk youth, and apparently he used that charity as a way to gain the trust of children he then molested.

I couldn't understand it. I'd never heard a whisper about it. Not one word. How could our football program get hit with something that terrible, that huge, something that had gone on for that long while he was an employee of the university and long afterward, when as far as I knew none of us players had any hint that anything was going on before the news broke that day? How were there no rumors? How was there no warning that there was an investigation underway? Nothing.

The commentators on TV started asking who was to blame for this going unreported for so long, saying the university president might be held accountable and insinuating that Joe Paterno must have known too. "How could he not know?" they said.

The Joe Paterno I knew was a man of integrity. A man of discipline. He didn't have tolerance for bad behavior. He'd kicked more than one player off the team for bad behavior off the field while I was at Penn State, and that bad behavior wasn't anywhere near as bad as something like this—targeting kids. He was a reasonable man too. He'd respected my opinion when I argued to bring one of those players back and give him a second chance. But there's no way anyone would have got a third chance with Joe. His team ran like clockwork—assistant coaches included.

If these allegations about Sandusky were true, which it sure seemed like they were given all the details that were on the news, I just couldn't believe that Joe might've known what was going on and still allowed Jerry Sandusky anywhere near his program, let alone his locker room.

The next morning Joe brought the whole team together for a squad meeting. The feeling in the room was awful. We just didn't know what was gonna happen. The media was speculating that he might get fired. But Joe stood up in front of the room and told us not to worry. He said he wasn't going anywhere, and that he'd for sure be there the whole rest of the season. "Focus on football," he said. "Focus on school."

But I looked around, and it seemed like the coaches were falling apart. Assistant coach Mike McQueary was taking it especially hard. He was apparently an eyewitness in the case. He had walked in on Sandusky one time back in 2002 and caught him in the showers with a young boy. And right after Joe's meeting, he held a separate meeting with his receivers. He clearly knew what was going on behind the scenes with the whole legal case and everything, and as soon as his meeting with the receivers was over, he told me that he'd broken down and cried as he spoke to them.

Somehow JoePa's assurances didn't seem so reassuring anymore.

*This is about to get real,* I thought. To me, a grown man crying in front of his players meant something crazy was about to happen.

The next morning, November 8, the university president canceled Joe's weekly press conference. We had a game against Nebraska coming up that weekend, and we always held press conferences to talk football. Not scandals. *Football.* No one could understand why that press conference got canceled. A bunch of students rallied in front of JoePa's house that night, just to show their support for the man, and the police showed up to break up the crowd. In

Happy Valley! There wasn't any violence. It wasn't a mob scene. Why would the cops show up?

The mood all over campus got real tense after that. It's like no one knew what to do. There was no guidance. No direction. There were cameras everywhere from national news outlets, all the big networks, ESPN, reporters from all kinds of publications trying to get into the Lasch Building. Some of those reporters looked like college students themselves, and some of them tried to nonchalantly sneak in behind us when us players opened the doors with our access keys. We had to post people at the doors full time to let us in and out and keep the press out.

These aren't the kinds of situations that a team prepares for, and definitely not something any team should have to deal with in the middle of a season. How were we supposed to get ready for our game when all this was going on? How were we supposed to function when we kept hearing more and more details about how many kids had been hurt by this monster who'd been hanging around our weight room?

The stress of it all was intense, and none of us had any idea when or how it was all gonna end. The school didn't provide us with counselors or anything, or give us any guidance about it as a team. It's like we were all just left to deal with it in our own way.

When Joe called another squad meeting on the morning of November 9, we all got real nervous. It was dead quiet when he walked in through the side door like he always did. He was dressed in his gray sweater with a white collared shirt underneath it, with tan pants that were rolled up at the bottom revealing his white socks, and black shoes with white shoestrings—just like he always was. And he got behind the podium and coughed a little bit, like he always did just before he spoke.

But when he opened his mouth, everything was different.

He sounded hesitant. Confused, almost. And in so many words, he told us that he had decided to retire at the end of the season.

The whole team gasped. No one could believe it. This man had been coaching at Penn State for more than sixty years, as head coach for forty-six. JoePa wasn't the sort of man who "retires." He would die on the field if he could. He'd lived and breathed Penn State football for three-quarters of his life on this earth. Penn State was the lifeblood that ran through his veins. For him to up and decide to retire after telling us he wasn't going anywhere just a couple of days earlier, that man must've been under enormous pressure, the likes of which none of us can possibly imagine.

He kept his remarks real short, and then he turned to go. But when he reached the doorway, he paused. He stopped and looked back at us with tears in his eyes. I'll never forget that look. That wasn't the look of a man who was planning to be out on the practice field the next day. That wasn't the look of a man who had half a season left to coach. It wasn't the look of a man who had a shot at winning his 410th game that coming weekend.

It was the look of a man who was saying goodbye for good.

Sure enough, just after 10:30 that night, the news broke all over the TV: Joe Paterno, one of the greatest coaches in college football history, got fired. The university didn't even fire him face-to-face. They fired him when he was sitting at home getting ready to go to bed. They fired him over the phone.

The shock of it was too much to take. The whole campus erupted with anger and confusion. Students poured into the streets, and the media was right there to capture it all. Once again, police showed up—this time in huge numbers and dressed in riot gear—and that seemed to make matters worse. Some people in the crowd got violent. People started flipping cars over and all sorts of craziness went down. I wouldn't call it a "riot" like the police and the media kept calling it. I would just call it confusion. It was a bunch of confused college kids who didn't understand what was going on, who were responding to the sudden, disrespectful firing of one of our school's most respected and revered men. To most students, Joe Paterno *was* Penn State.

I was glad I lived off campus that night. I was glad I didn't get caught up in all of that confusion. I was glad to be at home, alone, where I could gather my thoughts and think about how to respond. After all, I had to keep my head on straight about this. I had to keep some perspective. I had to think about what this meant for our team and our future. I had a role to play now.

I was team captain for a football team that suddenly had no head coach.

I prayed to God that night. I prayed that Joe Paterno would get through this. I prayed for his family. I prayed for the victims. Then I prayed to God for Penn State. Our community. Our campus.

When I set aside the anger and confusion in my mind, I could make sense of the school asking Joe to step down. These charges were terrible. They were serious. We're talking about *kids*. I'm a father. I understood that there had to be consequences. Joe Paterno was Sandusky's supervisor. Even if he didn't know about any of it, he *should have known*. Especially if it was happening under his watch.

As a leader you have to be willing to take the credit, whether good or bad.

Still, I could not and will never understand how the leaders at the top of our school could be so disrespectful as to fire him—a man who'd been there for decades, who was personally responsible for so much of the reputation and stature of that school—with no warning and over the phone. That just wasn't right. And that made me angry.

But this unrest, this insanity that erupted on the streets and sidewalks of our campus—that wasn't right either. We couldn't let this scandal pull us apart. That isn't what Joe Paterno would want to see happen to Penn State, and he certainly wouldn't want this scandal to pull his team apart. His legacy needed to go on and go on strong.

The last thing that needed to happen was for us to let the team or the campus community fall apart. What we needed was to pull together. And after praying about it, I had an idea.

I called a squad meeting the next day.

I looked my teammates in the eye one by one as I spoke.

"We're all hurting right now," I said. "But we can't fall apart. We can't let this scandal divide us. We can't let this scandal divide our campus and redefine who we are. All those cameras out there, it's like they're just waitin' for us to mess up. They're just waitin' on us to keep rioting so they can show it on the news. It's like they want us to fall apart or something, to take us down. But we're not gonna let that happen."

"No," some of the guys responded.

"We got senior day tomorrow, and we seniors—we've been here a long time. We've paid our dues. We built our careers on JoePa's leadership."

A few of my fellow seniors and fifth-year seniors shouted, "Yes!"

"We need to make Joe Paterno proud. We need to make Penn State proud. We need to show the world that this scandal will not define us and will not rip us apart."

"*Yes!*"

"So here's what I'm thinking. We're not gonna run out of that tunnel tomorrow as a bunch of individuals like we usually do," I said. "Tomorrow, when we come out of that tunnel, we're gonna walk out of that tunnel as one. We're gonna link arms, as one team, and show the whole world the true meaning of 'We Are!'"

The reaction from my teammates was almost hushed. A few of them started nodding their heads and smiling a bit, like they got it. "Yeah." Like they really got that we had a role to play here. This wasn't about football. This was about a way that we could symbolically show the whole world that we were united during this awful time.

A couple of the assistant coaches patted me on the back as that meeting ended. I think they hoped, like I did, that this gesture could help bring the school community together and put an end to the campus unrest.

That night there was some more trouble around campus. A bunch of students continued to turn their anger outward, even as another group of students held a candlelight vigil for the victims of Jerry Sandusky's crimes. *That's* where the focus should've been. All those children. All those families who'd been hurt by that man. But we were a campus divided by pain and confusion. The healing couldn't start in earnest until we came together.

The next day, November 12, under bright blue skies, I led our team onto the football field linked arm and arm with Derek Moye, Quinn Barham, and Drew Astorino. Four across. The whole team linked arms in rows of four behind us as we walked out of the tunnel through a human corridor created by the band on one side and the Football Letterman's Club on the other—and a stadium full of 106,000 people fell silent. You could've heard a pin drop.

Everywhere I looked, I saw people dressed not only in Penn State colors, dark blue and white, but also wearing shirts and body paint that said "We (heart) JoePa" or "Thank You Joe." I knew then and there that his legacy would be all right. But I don't think it's a coincidence that dark blue is a color that's often associated with causes that support victims of child sexual abuse. It was just too big to be a coincidence to me. This was something more. Like I said, this was about much more than football.

People wore dark-blue ribbons pinned to their shirts. They had dark-blue ribbons painted on their faces. A whole section of students in dark-blue shirts formed the shape of a ribbon in the stands. Clearly I wasn't the only person on campus looking to do something to symbolically pull us all together. Other leaders-in-waiting all across that community stepped up and took charge too. And when we met Nebraska's team at midfield to take a knee in a moment of silence for the victims of these atrocities, the whole world saw that. The whole world was watching. Because this wasn't just a football game. This was healing. It was a chance to turn our collective attention away from the scandal, the gossip, the pain of what that one man had caused, which then rippled through an entire football program and college campus. It was a chance to turn our attention to victims of child sexual abuse—not just here at Penn State, but *everywhere.*

I don't understand the way God works sometimes. I certainly didn't pretend to understand much about God at all as a fifth-year senior at Penn State University. But on that day, kneeling in that stadium, in that silence, surrounded by tens of thousands of people dressed in solidarity in dark blue, I looked around, and I felt God at work.

Our team didn't win that football game. We played well, and I think we did JoePa proud considering the circumstances. But Nebraska beat us.

We won regardless.

Our team and our campus turned a corner that day. There were no more riots after that. The healing had begun.

# CHAPTER NINE

# ROAD GAMES

>> At our next game, the very next week, I blew out my back.

It happened during warm-ups, during takeoffs. We were playing Ohio State. Our biggest rival. There were NFL scouts at the game. I didn't want anyone to see me hurting, so I tried to play it off like it was no big deal. I could barely walk, though, and Coach Johnson gave me a look of concern. He asked me if I was okay, and I told him, "No."

I went into the locker room looking for help. The scandal was still fresh on everyone's minds. I was the leader of the team. I didn't think I could afford to take time off. I believed that I needed to be out there for the team, for the university, *and* for my future.

So, I let them put a shot in my back to block the pain. It was like some *Varsity Blues*–type stuff where I no longer felt the pain, but I knew I was messed up. I knew it was serious. I went out there and played and ignored it anyway. I played strong, and so did the rest of the team. We won: 20–14. And we kept on playing strong in game after game during that first-ever post-Paterno era. I pushed aside the pain, I even sat out practices just to stay strong enough for games, but I pressed forward for the sake of our school, our team, and my future.

I spent time on Skype with my daughter every week, but I missed her. A part of me worried that she might not recognize me anymore or something. Or worse, that she might not light up when I walked in the room.

Because her mom had moved so far away, I'd missed Leah's first steps. I'd only heard her talking full words through a phone. I hated that she was so far away from me. I loved that girl so much, and I needed to get her back in my life. I knew I needed to stay focused on football so I could make that happen.

My parents were still making the effort to come to every single one of my games, even when they were in relationships with other people and had totally separate lives. My mother would tell me my dad drove her nuts! But she seemed able to laugh about it and move past it; and my dad seemed to move past all of his differences with her, too, just to show up and sit in the stadium and watch me play. I prayed that Leah's mom and I might be able to do that for Leah at some point.

As the football season wound down, all signs pointed to me making all of my dreams and ambitions come true. Becoming an All-American. Winning awards. Landing a top spot in the NFL Draft. All of it looked like it was right there for me, right around the corner. I just had to make it through December without my back injury getting in the way. I thought that was my only obstacle.

I was wrong.

When the first All-American list came out—the Coaches' list—my name wasn't on it.

My record was solid. There was no disputing that I was one of the top, if not *the* top, defensive linemen in all of college football. I knew for sure there wasn't anyone in college football who didn't know my name. Which meant there was only one reason why my name wasn't on that list, and that's because Penn State was caught up in scandal. It seemed clear to me that none of the other coaches in college football wanted anything about that scandal to come anywhere near them, and that's why they left me and any other Penn State players off their list.

I had no idea the repercussions of the scandal would affect me personally.

I went fuming into a meeting room with my defensive line coach and our assistant defensive line coach the day the list came out, and they seemed to concur that the whole thing was BS.

"I feel like I'm being punished, like we're all being punished, for something that had nothing to do with us, that happened before any of us on this team even came to this school!" I said.

They tried to calm me down, but they clearly felt the same way.

"Just keep working and don't let it get to you," they said. "Just keep working hard."

I listened to them. If I didn't listen, I might have lost focus and not played my best in the games that followed. But I listened. I did what Joe Paterno always told us to do: "Focus on football." And guess what? Every All-American list that came out after that, I was on. Despite the scandal, despite losing Joe Paterno as our coach, I wound up heading toward the end of the season as a consensus All-American. If the Coaches' list would have included me, I would have been one of only eight unanimous All-Americans that year.

The Coaches' list wasn't the last of the fallout, though. As team captain, I was essentially put in front of the media week after week as team spokesperson. We had games every week, and I was traveling around to awards ceremonies in between, and everywhere I went the press wanted to know details about the team and the scandal and how we were adjusting without Paterno at the helm—and nobody from Penn State gave me any guidance on how to handle that. They didn't give me any media training. They didn't sit me down and tell me what to say or not to say. I had to figure it all out on my own. Talk about education by fire! No matter what the media wanted to know—and they definitely seemed to want to dig deep into some personal and private matters concerning the school and the locker rooms and the coaches—I found a way to turn the conversation back to football; to let them know that our Penn State family was strong, and we were gonna stay strong.

I was a fifth-year senior. I was still a college kid. It wasn't my job to handle all that additional stress. I just wanted to play football and go to classes and live my life. Why would the school leave me so vulnerable like that? Was it on purpose? Did they trust me as a leader to go out there and say and do the right things, just based on my reputation? Because I certainly didn't feel prepared for all that. Or was it just an oversight? Did nobody prepare me because they were too focused on themselves? I'll never know. I just did the best I could, and by the time the season was over I felt like somebody ought to have added a "Minor in Media Training" line to my official college transcript.

I still don't know how I managed to deal with all of that pressure, other than the fact that I knew I needed to persevere through absolutely *everything* if I wanted to make it to the NFL. I couldn't get derailed. I only had one shot at this.

Maybe having big goals was an even bigger deal than I knew, because having those goals in place, all driven by the desire to make a better life for my daughter, is absolutely what helped me focus.

I wound up winning the MVP award at Penn State that season. My parents were in the audience, and my dad came up to me after my speech with this look on his face that was beyond proud. It's like he was astounded for some reason.

"Devon," he said. "Where did you learn to speak like that?"

"What do you mean?"

"I've never seen you give a speech before. The way you controlled the crowd—they laughed when you wanted them to laugh, and they hushed down when you wanted them to be serious. It's like every emotion you wanted to pull from this crowd, you did! They were hanging on your every word. That's something special."

I hadn't thought about how much my speaking might have improved. I'd been doing it all season, over and over, not just in the locker room but in front of press audiences big and small. I didn't think of it as a skill I had developed, but clearly my father was impressed.

Winning MVP after going through all of the struggle that season felt great. And now I had a shot at the Outland Trophy—the award that goes to the best lineman in college football. I was nominated against a player from Alabama who I'd crushed in one of my best games of the season. That Alabama game was the one I personally felt made me an All-American–worthy player, and that game very clearly put me ahead of that Alabama player. So, I was real excited about the possibility of taking that trophy home.

Me and my dad got all dressed up to attend the ESPN College Football Awards show that year, where that trophy would get handed out. To be able to take my dad to an event like that full of cameras and a red carpet and everything, after all those years, all that effort, knowing all the sacrifices he'd made to get me to that point in my career—it brings tears to my eyes just thinking about it.

When it came time to hand out the Outland Trophy, I could barely contain myself. A cameraman came right up and pointed the camera in my face, just waiting for the big moment.

"And the Outland Trophy goes to . . ." the announcer said as he opened the envelope. But then he looked over the top of his glasses, right at me, and then right at my dad, and he looked back at the card and he read the Alabama player's name.

I couldn't react. I had a camera in my face. I was supposed to clap and smile and be happy for that guy, and that's what I did for the camera—but I was *crushed*.

"God, please," I prayed, "please tell me this scandal is not going to overshadow and erase all of the things that I've accomplished and all that I've overcome. Please!"

That award should've been mine. I knew it. My dad knew it. My coaches knew it. The announcer knew it. He gave us that look for a reason. I tried to let that thought comfort me. "Okay, people know that I deserved that award. I may not have gotten it, but people know it."

Even as we were leaving town, we kept running into other players and coaches at the airport who said, "Man, you had one heck of a year. Just keep focusing and keep fighting."

But it kept happening. I was named Big Ten Defensive Player of the Year, which was huge for me, but then I wasn't even nominated for the Lombardi Award, which goes to the best defensive player in the country. These decisions clearly weren't about me. They were about politics. It was about people trying to keep their awards away from a scandal that rocked college football. I kept getting angry about it, yet I had to keep trying to find a way to make peace with it. I tried to keep telling myself, "People know what I'm all about. People know my record. So none of this will affect my position in the NFL Draft."

At Penn State, I was the number-one pick out of our class. Everyone knew that. I had to hold tight to that thought and believe it would all work out okay.

The Draft wouldn't happen until April 2012, though. I still had work to do. We had Bowl Season ahead.

Oh, yeah. And I had to graduate. My graduation day that December came right in the middle of all of this, right before Christmas break. Graduating in December isn't like graduating in the spring. It happens indoors instead of out on the fields. It's a much smaller ceremony. My mind was so focused on other things that for me it went by in a blur. But for my parents? That day was something special. My dad told me it was one of the proudest moments of his life. I was the first person in our entire family to graduate from college. My brother went ahead of me and served as an inspiration to me to want to go, but he didn't make it to graduation after starting a family himself. He and his girlfriend had twins during his college years. So he had come close, but he didn't get to wear that cap and gown.

When I put on that cap and gown and accepted my diploma, I was opening up a whole new world for my family. It's like I had broken the cycle. My little sister would eventually graduate from college. And I couldn't imagine that Leah wouldn't go to college too. It would be sort of automatic now, wouldn't it? Graduating college would go from the exception in our family to the standard.

"My son, a college graduate. With a degree in criminal justice, no less," my dad said while giving me a great big hug after the ceremony. He was practically glowing with pride. "Could you have even imagined this day back in the fifth grade when I brought you to jail?"

"No, Dad. No. Although that might be where my interest in criminal justice first got started, you know?" I said with a laugh.

"Well just think, if I hadn't had them throw you in a cell for a couple of hours, where would you be right now?"

"Wait, *you* did that?" I asked.

"Yeah! I thought you knew," he said.

"I sort of suspected after a while, but you never told me," I said.

"Yeah, that was me. Just trying to set you straight."

I paused for a second and took it all in.

"Thank you," I said. "Thank you for being there for me. I wouldn't be here if it wasn't for you."

Tears started to well up in his eyes, and in mine, as we just stayed there in that moment, living the dream.

• • •

There's a strange period at the end of a senior's final football season when everyone knows which players are headed for the NFL, but under NCAA rules, no one's supposed to pursue it. There are all sorts of scouts and recruiters around, sports agents trying to befriend the best prospects, and marketing agents looking to unofficially sign lucrative deals with the players they think might have the brightest futures.

I was caught up in all of that. After the season I'd had, it was clear that I was wanted—and my brother, Tony, stepped in to help sort it all out while I kept my head focused on the game.

Despite having an amazing season, a season that would have been worthy of sending us to one of the big New Year's Day bowl games in any other year, our team got picked for the TicketCity Bowl—on the Monday *after* New Year's Day. A game that practically nobody would be watching.

There was no question in anyone's mind that it was a purposeful slight. It felt to me like the NCAA wanted to hide Penn State from public view because of the school's now negative image. And the team was sick and tired of it. In fact, my teammates all wanted to boycott the game in protest of the unfair treatment we'd suffered since the scandal broke.

That rattled the coaching staff. They didn't know what to do. They didn't have Joe Paterno to give them direction, so they turned to me. They pulled me into a meeting. "We can't just have our team not show up!" they said. "Convince them. Convince the rest of the guys that boycotting is the wrong thing to do."

Honestly, I wasn't sure that it was the wrong thing to do. We worked hard and we deserved a better bowl. We'd been given the short end of the stick. Did anyone from this university even stick up for us?

In the meantime, the powers in charge at Penn State hired a new athletic director, and this man who we didn't even know came into one of our squad meetings and tried to strong-arm us. "You're all going to the bowl game whether you like it or not," he said.

He wound up getting into a back-and-forth shouting match with one of our linebackers.

I'd had about enough at that point.

I stood up in that squad meeting and said, "Look, if you're going to come in here and address us in a squad meeting, you need to address us like men. We're not little kids who you can order around, and what the university is going through is not our fault. We feel like nobody is sticking up for us, while people out there are looking at us as if we had something to do with this scandal. Maybe if you all came at us like grown men and understood our point of view, then maybe we might plan a bowl game. But you can't force us to do anything!"

He backed down a bit after that, but my teammates still didn't want to play that game. I wrestled with what to do. I had all kinds of people in my ear telling me to let it go. "You don't want to go play that game anyway. You can't risk getting injured. There's a lot of money on the line, and right now, you're expected to be picked in the top twenty!" they said.

Nobody knew I'd been fighting a back injury most of the season. Nobody knew I'd torn my rotator cuff that season as well. All season long I'd been hiding that injury. I couldn't let anyone in the NFL know I wasn't in top shape. That's the way it is for the top college players all over this country. It's brutal, but it's part of the grind if you want to make it to the top.

I knew how much was on the line for me personally, but I felt that this wasn't about me. This was about my team. This was about Penn State and the legacy of the program Joe Paterno created. I just couldn't let my team come off to the world like a bunch of quitters. Not now. Not after all we'd been through together. So, I ended up calling another squad meeting.

"Look," I said, "I'm the number-one pick out of this class right now, and I'm willing to risk *everything* for you all to go out there and play one more time with you—because if we give up right now, then we're basically telling the Penn State community that it's okay to give up and just quit."

As a leader, I felt I had no choice but to put the university and team before myself—and it worked. Everyone got on board.

I broke my toe a couple of days before the bowl game at practice doing one-on-ones. Our defensive coordinator, who'd been promoted to the role of head coach in Joe's absence, told me to take the rest of the week off—but he needed me to play. I wasn't sure I could. I could barely walk. But I couldn't talk the team into going to the bowl and just back out. I wound up getting a shot again so I could play through the pain.

I didn't play like my normal self that game, but I left what I had on the field for my last time in the Blue and White.

We lost that game. But we proved we weren't quitters.

Was it worth it? I think so. But the personal sacrifice I made took a toll.

Once the shot wore off, I couldn't run anymore. I could barely walk on it. It was January, and I couldn't train the way I needed to for the upcoming NFL Combine in February.

Another setback. A setback that made me question whether I should have slowed down and asked God for more guidance. Had I pushed too far? Was it really my role to go out there and play that game and risk so much for the sake of my team?

Something magical happened in the final seconds of that game though. Something that would change my life. What I wouldn't realize until afterward was that once that bowl game was over, once that clock hit zero on the very last game of my college career, I was no longer held back by NCAA guidelines. I was free to pursue my professional career. I was free to go get endorsement deals and everything else that college players aren't allowed to do.

So, the moment the clock hit zero in that game, the marketing team my brother had agreed to sign me with wired $100,000 to my bank account. A hundred-thousand-dollar marketing advance. My bank account that had maybe fifteen dollars in it before that moment was suddenly flush with cash.

When I looked at the balance on the banking app on my phone, it made me burst out crying. I couldn't believe it. My mom and my dad and my brother were at that game, and the first thing I did was to offer to help them all out with some of their bills. I owed them all so much, and I knew this was just the beginning.

I wound up flying to Miami to train for the Combine, and landing in Miami at age twenty-one with $100,000 in the bank was a trip. I'd never had *any* money. I couldn't go out much because of my injuries and because I needed to try to train—in the weight room if nothing else—but just knowing that I could go out to a restaurant or a club if I wanted to made me feel rich.

The best part about it was I got to do some nice things for my family. I flew my mom, my little sister, and Leah all down to Miami together. So they got to hang out in the sunshine by a pool all day while I worked out.

"I like palm trees even better than Christmas trees!" Leah told me one day.

She was *three*. I didn't see a palm tree in real life until I started traveling to bowl games in college. I loved that she was getting so much experience in the world and living without blinders from the start. And my mom? She settled right in, with her sunglasses and bathing suit and bleach-blonde hair. You would've thought she'd been coming to Miami her whole life, and she loved being "Mom-Mom" to Leah. She took to it all like a fish to water.

Leah loved the pool. I had put her in swimming lessons the year before that, not knowing that she'd wind up in Miami a year later, swimming all day in a luxurious hotel pool. Here I was a grown man who still didn't know how to swim, who'd never had the opportunity to learn how to swim, and my little girl was splashing around with no fear at all.

Money doesn't buy health, though. Even though I took it easy on my foot and my shoulder and worked with some great trainers to push my body everywhere else I could, my body was still a mess at the end of January. I had to flat-out skip the 2012 Nike Senior Bowl exhibition game, which is a huge part of the annual scouting season. I know that hurt me, big time, because I had coaches and press people telling me they wished they'd seen me at that game.

Instead of training for the Combine drills like everyone else, I spent all those weeks seeing doctors, trying to fix my back, toe, and shoulder. Up until a week before the Combine, I couldn't bench more than 135 pounds.

When it came time for the NFL Combine that February, I pushed through the pain and gave it my all. I had no choice. At the start, when they checked everybody's physical condition, there were doctors pulling on my toes and yanking on my shoulder, and I just breathed real deep and played it off like it didn't hurt one bit. I made it through some of the early drills just fine too. But after we got through the 40-yard dash, which is one of the most-watched drills of that whole event, my foot hurt real bad. I basically wound up walking behind all the other players for the rest of that day, skipping a whole bunch of drills, and I think that gave the wrong impression. I think some of the coaches thought I was acting like I was too good to perform drills like everybody else.

I couldn't let them know it was because I had a broken toe.

All I could do was wait until April and hope my record at Penn State was enough to keep me up at the top of the Draft—and I had every assurance from people around me that it would.

This was it. My dream of getting to the NFL was coming true. And after all I'd gone through, I felt like that dream was close enough to start celebrating. I flew back to Miami to keep training—and I invited a few of my old friends to fly down and join me. What good is having money in the bank if you can't enjoy some of it, right?

We spent the better part of the next month living it up. And it was *fun*. To be in that city of all cities, after everything we'd grown up with—it felt like the gates had opened to all of us seeing a different side of life that we'd never known. People in that town knew who I was. They knew I was headed to the Draft. So when we went out to clubs and restaurants, we got VIP treatment, like we were rappers or something, or like I'd made it in the NFL already. We became regulars at LIV, the massive, two-story, lit-up club at the Fontainebleau Hotel, with music thumping and gorgeous girls everywhere. They crammed like a thousand people into that place on Sunday nights. And at the end of the night, before everybody goes home, all this confetti falls from the ceiling as the lights swirl around. The first time it happened, I looked around at my friends, and we all felt like we were in that Mekhi Phifer movie, *Paid in Full*.

"This is the life," I shouted.

Then we all picked up our glasses and raised 'em high, as we all yelled together, "This is the life!"

# CHAPTER TEN

# THE DRAFT

>> I had dreamed of making it to the NFL Draft since I was in high school. In my mind, I'd heard the voice of the announcer calling my name. I'd pictured myself walking across that stage and shaking hands with the commissioner.

Now? It wasn't a dream. I was *there*. I'd done the work to get there. I'd overcome injuries and persevered through an unimaginable scandal. I'd made it. I was in New York City ready to find out where my future would take me, ready to make my NFL fantasy come true, ready to give my all to whichever team wanted me.

The energy of the event in New York that day was insane. It was more powerful than I ever could have imagined. All of the top players from all of the big schools were corralled backstage in the green room, standing by with their agents and coaches and parents, all waiting for our futures to be decided, waiting for our big moment. These were my peers now. This is where I belonged.

I stood there surrounded by the best of the best young football players in the whole country. And I watched as one by one, thirty-two of their names got called—and mine didn't. Thirty-two of my peers each made a spot onto one of the thirty-two NFL teams in the first round. But not me.

I had never experienced what it felt like to be the kid in gym class who didn't get picked for a team. In fact, I'd mostly been the guy the gym teacher picked to do the picking. I'd grown used to being a leader. The team captain, even. And I thought I'd proven beyond a shadow of doubt that I belonged in that role during my time at Penn State. But as day one of the NFL Draft came to a close and I stood there with the remaining handful of players who didn't get picked that day, I felt like a loser.

I knew in my heart it wasn't my fault. Even the fact that I had ongoing injuries and missed the Senior Bowl, that was all part of the fallout from the stress and pressure that the Sandusky scandal added to my final season. But I could not understand why. *Why?* Why did this happen to me? How could this possibly be the result of all the hard work I'd put in, all the injuries I'd overcome, and the sacrifices I'd made by stepping into a leadership role under some of the most trying circumstances imaginable?

My agent spent the whole afternoon on the phone trying to get some answers, and another well-respected agent told my dad that I probably wouldn't get picked in the second round either. People were saying I might be bumped down to a third- or fourth-round pick!

I was back in my hotel room, lying on the bed trying to make sense of it all when my dad gave me that news, and I rolled over and threw a pillow across the room. I'm not a violent person. I never tended toward fits of rage. But that pillow knocked a lamp off the table and shattered it all over the floor, and I didn't even care that I'd damaged someone else's property. None of this made sense. I felt my dream slipping away, and it wasn't even my fault!

My parents and the rest of my family kept trying to calm me down, while everyone else around me said I shouldn't go back to the Draft the next day. If I wasn't called in that second round, it would be far too embarrassing, they said, and far too painful. I'd be better off sitting and waiting at home to get a call if it was gonna happen, they all said. We were all caught up in the emotions of the moment.

I just couldn't do it. I got downright stubborn about it. I'd dreamed of getting to the NFL Draft. I'd dreamed of walking across that stage. I couldn't let that go. I couldn't give it up. I was gonna show up and make it happen by sheer force of will.

The next day, I showed up in the green room for the second round, and it was only like me and a handful of other players back there. A lot of people opted for the stay-home-by-the-phone option. It was depressing. Out front, in front of the stage, there was still all kinds of energy and excitement. But backstage, after what we'd experienced the day before, it was kinda sad.

Before the event started, I came close to leaving. I came close to walking away and going home to wait by the phone just like everybody told me. But at that point, my parents told me to stick it out.

"Come on now, Devon," my mom said. "You were stubborn enough to bring us all back here today. Just stick around. Maybe you were right. Maybe this is your time."

I looked over at my baby girl, and she smiled. Leah was right there with my family, all dressed up cute, and I couldn't help but smile back. The sight of her smile was enough to lift me out of anything.

I stuck around as the thirty-third pick was made. And the thirty-fourth. And the thirty-fifth. . . .

I sat there and sat there on a cold metal chair with my head in my hands, letting pick after pick pound into my skull, watching it unfold on television monitors when all I wanted was to get out on that stage.

And the forty-ninth pick . . . And the fiftieth . . .

I thought maybe my turn wasn't gonna come.

And the fifty-first . . .

There were only two players left in the green room at this point. The whole room had emptied out. It was just me and a kid from LSU.

And the fifty-second. . . .

Just then my cell phone rang. I picked it up. It was Marvin Lewis, head coach of the Cincinnati Bengals, telling me to get ready because they were picking me next!

"Thank you, sir. Thank you."

My dad came over and put his hands on my shoulders. He could tell I was excited. He knew this was about to get real. We looked up at the monitors, and the man who stepped up to the podium to make the next announcement was wide receiver Isaac Curtis, the fifteenth overall pick by the Cincinnati Bengals back in the 1973 Draft. He stood there all dignified in his suit and tie, and my heart started pounding as he started to speak. I started sweating all over.

"With the fifty-third pick in the 2012 NFL Draft," he said, "the Cincinnati Bengals select . . . Devon Still. Defensive tackle. Penn State."

I stood up and I hugged my dad as a cameraman came right up to capture the moment. Then I turned, and my mom handed me Leah. I looked into that little smiling face of hers and knew that her life was gonna be something else. Her life just got better, and she didn't even know it. I hugged her tight, knowing that she was too young to know what this meant for us.

Then I hugged my mom, and my mom *knew*. She knew what this meant. Not just for me, but for all of us. So we hugged for a long, long time.

I knew they were waiting for me out on that stage, but I wasn't gonna let anyone rush this moment. As I held my mom and she started crying, I couldn't hold back the emotion. I started crying too. Then I hugged my little sister, who was all smiles, and a whole bunch of other people who'd supported me along the way. And then I finally made my way out onto the stage where I shook NFL Commissioner Roger Goodell's hand and gave him a big ol' hug, just like I'd envisioned doing for all those years. Just like I'd seen so many now-famous players do on TV over the years.

We posed for pictures and then I did a live TV interview with sideline reporter Melissa Stark. She asked me about how agonizing it was to wait backstage through the whole first day and so much of the second round, and I honestly felt like none of that mattered anymore. Why had I been so angry? What did it matter that I had to wait? I'd made it! There are so few players in the world who make it to the NFL, and I was one of them. That was a blessing, and I said so right there on live television.

As we were wrapping up the interview, though, she said something that hit me. She said how I'd now be playing with one of the top defensive lines in all of football. And then she said something like, "Well, now you'll be out there chasing Roethlisberger and Flacco. Good luck to you!"

This wasn't a dream anymore. This was a dream come true. This was *real*. Melissa Stark wasn't playing. The next time I went for a sack in the next official game I played, I could very well be aiming to take down one of the great quarterbacks of all time. This was my life now. That's where I was headed. I wasn't just a football player anymore. I was an NFL player. A Cincinnati Bengal. This was crazy!

As I made my way back to the green room, I caught sight of my dad's face. And I know he said that seeing me graduate college was the most proud he'd ever been, but I think this day had to have been his most exciting. I was the one feeling proud, knowing that he'd watched football all his life and tuned into the NFL Draft every year, and that as his son I'd now been able to let him experience that moment firsthand. I wouldn't trade that experience for the world— which is crazy since there was a point where we almost walked away from being there in person. If I'd been in the living room getting that phone call from the Bengals, it would not have been the same. I wouldn't have known what it felt like to walk across that stage. I only got to experience that because we stayed, even though people were telling us not to. And I knew, looking at my dad's face, that regardless of how my NFL career turned out, whatever I had to go through, nobody could ever take that feeling away. Nobody.

Before we left the building that day, I held Leah in my arms again. I looked into her smiling face, and I knew that it was all for her. I also knew what this *meant* for her.

• • •

Now it was *really* time to celebrate. In early May, I threw a big Draft party at a club in Philadelphia. We rented the whole place out just for me and my friends, and my friends' friends, and we blew the place up. I felt like a king or something. There were so many people there from my past, and people I didn't know, and all these girls trying to hang out with me and give me their number. It was crazy to think how fast my life had changed—after all those years of preparing to make it, ain't nobody prepared for what it's like. I just stood there wide-eyed, taking it all in, and still feeling like I was in a movie sometimes.

At one point my friend Charlie introduced me to a girl from Wilmington. Her name was Asha, and she was real pretty—but the party was so crazy I didn't really take notice of her at first. We started talking over the loud music, and she said she only lived about five minutes from where I grew up. We went to a lot of the same parties and knew a whole bunch of the same people, but for some reason we'd never crossed paths before that night.

"Maybe it's cause I don't really follow sports," she said.

"Oh really? Why you at this party then?" I asked her.

"Because my friend asked me to come, so I came!" she said.

I thought it was funny. There were all these people trying to get into that party just to get close to me, Mr. NFL Draft pick, and this Asha girl didn't even know who I was. We talked a little bit about the neighborhoods we were both familiar with, and then somehow it came up that we had the same birthday. She didn't believe me, so I had to show her my license. She laughed and her eyes lit up and her smile jolted my heart. There were so many people at this party that I got pulled away and soon lost track of her. But then toward the end of the night, she came up to me again. "Hey, that girl over there wants your number," she said. I looked over at the girl, and something in my mind said not to do it.

"I don't want to give her my number," I said.

"Why not?" she asked.

"I want *your* number."

Asha turned her head to the side and looked a little taken aback. "My number?" she said.

"Yeah. Can I call you?"

She looked at me again like I was a little bit crazy. But then she smiled. "Give me your phone," she said, and I handed it to her. She punched in her digits. I said, "Thank you," and I'm sure she walked away thinking she'd never hear from me again.

She was right, at least for a while. I was too busy to call her. But that didn't mean I wasn't thinking about her. I don't know what it was, but I could not get Asha off my mind.

Riding the highs from that party and all the rest of the fun and attention that came with being an NFL player, I flew out to Cincinnati right after that and got thrown right into rookie mini-camp practice. My body wasn't fully healed yet. My back felt better, but my toe was still messed up. It didn't matter. I crushed it. I could not be blocked. It was almost easy for me. I expected going to the NFL would be a big step up, a whole new level of challenge, but this felt easier than college. One of the players I played with there, Carlos Dunlap, he came up to me and was like, "Man, you have everybody in here talking about why you should've been a first-round Draft pick."

That was some much-needed validation right there.

Because I was one of the newest members of the team, the Bengals put me up in front of the cameras at a press conference that first week in Cincinnati. It was kind of funny. One of the reporters asked who my favorite team was growing up, and I said, "The Steelers. Yeah, definitely. Mostly because they were my dad's favorite team."

Everyone looked kind of shocked. I didn't even think about the fact that the Steelers and the Bengals were big rivals. I just kept on talking. "Yeah, my dad says he brought me home from the hospital in a little Steelers jersey!"

I got a little talking to after that press conference, and I stopped talking positive about the Steelers after that. But it was all good. It was just me, and it was all the truth! We had a good laugh over it, and everyone on the team was feeling real good about my performance.

As we moved on to the veteran minicamp, though, I went to hit someone and I felt the same pop in my back that I'd experienced during the Ohio State game at Penn State. For three straight days I could barely walk. I hobbled around all hunched over, bent at the hip like an old man.

The team doctors said I might need disc surgery, and it hurt so bad I was ready to say yes. But then I happened to catch a segment on ESPN where someone was talking about back surgeries and how most people don't come back from them—especially the type of surgery they were talking about me having. There was no way I was gonna wind up losing my career when I'd barely begun my rookie year, so I asked about other options. The doctor suggested an epidural, which would numb the pain so that I could get out there and practice. I didn't care that playing with a spinal injury that was all numbed up might cause me to get hurt even worse somewhere down the line. There was no way I was going to let my career come to an end before it started. So I said yes.

There was something lurking in the background of all of this too. That same year, my buddy John's sixteen-year-old nephew got shot. The boy got killed back home, and John just about lost it. John had graduated college already, but he didn't get a chance to play for the NFL. And the death hit him real hard. "Is this what life is all about?" he said to me one time. "You just be here and die before you get to enjoy or even see a different side of life?"

He got real down after that. He'd moved back home to Wilmington and he'd started smoking and doing all sorts of things that weren't in line with what he ought to be doing. It was heartbreaking. John and I had been through a lot together. In fact, he was one of the friends who was in the car with us when the cops pulled us over that fateful night. I was worried about him. He stayed on my mind all the time, and when I prayed, I prayed that he'd be okay.

Thankfully John had a girlfriend (who would eventually become his wife) who brought him to church and helped him deal with it all. Over the course of that year he made a complete 180. He gave up his bad habits. He gave himself to God. He started teaching youth ministry. It was crazy. I'd grown up with this kid and knew what he was all about. He'd come from the roughest of neighborhoods and tended to hang around a lot of wrong people when our crew wasn't together. He got into way more trouble than I ever did at my worst. So, to witness his transformation into this straightlaced, upstanding, churchgoing man was astonishing to me.

While I was resting up myself, I finally got around to calling that girl who'd been on my mind since my Draft party: Asha. She was surprised to hear from me, and I apologized for waiting so long to call, but then we just started talking like we'd known each other our whole lives. Once we started talking, we talked all the time.

I got back to Delaware briefly that June, and we went on our first few dates before I had to get back to training camp. Even after just that short time spent together, I felt like this might have a chance to turn into something special if we could just figure out how to get over the physical distance between us.

"I probably won't get back to Delaware until fall now," I told her. "We're just full time with practice and then the season starts in September."

"That's okay," she said. "I'm not going anywhere."

I looked forward to the day when we'd be able to spend some serious time together in person. But for now, I needed to concentrate on football.

Once I got back to practice full time, I could tell I wasn't playing my best, even with my pain all numbed up. My balance was a little off. My footing was a little off. But I stuck it out, and I played strong enough to stay on the roster.

Before I knew it, it was time for my very first game in the NFL: September 10, 2012, against the Ravens in their hometown Baltimore stadium. A Monday Night game. Watching the team come out of that tunnel with the smoke and the lights and the music, and watching Ray Lewis do that crazy pregame dance of his, I was like, *Wow. I know I'm supposed to be focused on the game, but I used to see this on TV when I was growing up. I can't believe I'm here. This is wild!*

My whole family was in the stands for that game, including my parents, side by side just like they'd sat in the stands for every game I'd ever played. Only this time, my mom had someone else with her: she brought Leah, all dressed up in a Bengals cheerleader outfit, and kept her on her lap. This was the start of a whole new era for me, and it was hard to imagine that this was actually the life Leah was gonna grow up knowing—sitting in stadiums, watching her daddy play in the NFL, not worrying about money all the time. She had so much promise in front of her that she didn't even know about yet.

Seeing her smile and wave at me filled my heart.

I only got in that first game for a handful of plays, and I definitely did not play my best. But I wasn't worried. I knew it would just take some time for me to settle in. I just kept praying that my back would heal up on its own in between epidurals. What mattered most is that I'd made it. I was playing in the NFL. I was living the dream. I was playing against the best of the best and holding my own at that level even though my body wasn't at its best. Week after week I looked around and took it all in and appreciated every second I was on those fields, in those stadiums, playing against players I'd grown up watching on TV.

I kept talking to Asha on the phone through all of it.

Our seventh game that season was against the Pittsburgh Steelers. My dad's favorite team. I'm not sure if he was rooting for us or against us, but I went out there and had one of my best games yet. In the second quarter I sacked their quarterback, Ben Roethlisberger, and he fumbled the ball. I'm still not sure if that made my dad proud or angry or a little of both, but I was pumped. It's hard to explain what it feels like to take down one of the giants of the game like that. Our team lost in the end, but I left that stadium feeling like I was back. Like I could do this for real. Like my whole future and Leah's whole future was opening up right in front of us.

That game happened right before our bye week, which meant I finally had a week off, and the timing could not have been more perfect. I went back to Wilmington and crashed at my dad's little apartment, and everywhere I went it seemed like everybody had watched that game. Even at the mall people were stopping me to ask what it felt like to sack Big Ben. "It felt great!" I said, laughing pretty much every time because it all still felt so surreal to me.

The funny thing is I didn't feel any different. I didn't feel famous. I just felt grateful. I'd picked up my first NFL-sized paychecks by then, and the first thing I did was start paying bills for everybody in my family. I didn't want them to worry anymore. They were the ones who got me where I was, and they deserved to enjoy some financial freedom because of it.

Leah's mom had moved back to Delaware at that point, which was great, because it meant my baby girl was right there smiling the moment I came home to visit.

We still talked and Skyped all the time, but there was nothing like getting back home and spending time just me and her. She was growing up so fast, and she just got to be more and more fun all the time. She was learning to sing her ABCs, and she loved playing games. We came up with our own handshake together, too, and it went like this: she would kiss my cheek, I would kiss hers, then she'd kiss my other cheek, and I would kiss hers, then she would kiss my forehead, and I would kiss hers, then we'd shake each other's hands.

We had so much fun together that we wore each other out. Sometimes she fell asleep in my arms on the couch at the end of the day. She was only the length of my arm from head to toe, but she had me wrapped around her finger. All she had to do was pout her little lips at me and I'd do anything for her.

That time off also gave me a chance to go out with Asha again. We wound up really getting to know each other once we were face-to-face, and I saw something in her that I wanted to be around all the time. Namely, a giving heart. Asha was always wanting to do things for other people, which is exactly how I wanted to be. She had goals and dreams. She was trained as a hairstylist, she'd gone to school for it, but she wanted to design her own products and have her own line of hair extensions someday. She had ambition. But at the root of all that ambition was this desire to make life better for everyone around her. She liked to focus on other people instead of focusing on herself. She wanted to help the people in her family. She wanted to help people in her community. I loved that. It was just so different than what I was seeing in all the typical girls who hung around and tried to get the attention of NFL players all the time.

I went back to Cincinnati thinking Asha was a girl I could get serious about. In fact, I went back to Cincinnati feeling on top of the world.

I jumped into our eighth game of the season against the Denver Broncos and played the best game of my NFL career so far. I had seven tackles, two solo, and two tackles for loss. I made the front page of the newspaper in Cincinnati. My teammates and the coaches were all joking around with me, like, "Don't let it go to your head!" But I was sure that my injuries were fully behind me and my career was about to take off.

I should've known better.

Life rarely moves in a straight line, and the pattern of my life seemed to be getting clearer and clearer: every time things were going my way, some new challenge came out of the blue.

The very next week, just before our game against the New York Giants, one of our veteran players came off IR (the injured/reserve list), and the team decided to dress him instead of me.

I got benched!

I could not believe my luck. Was this my version of the curse that seemed to be following me and my old high school teammates around? Was it just a coincidence? After all the injuries I'd endured and overcome, I just couldn't understand why these things kept happening to me. It didn't make any sense.

As soon as I had a chance, I pulled the head coach aside and asked him, "What's going on? I just had one of my best games. I made the front page of the paper. How come I got benched *now*?"

"You'll just have to wait your turn," he said.

An NFL team was only allowed to dress forty-six players per game. I was the new guy. The low man on the totem pole. But is seniority that only thing that matters in life?

I got benched the whole rest of the season through no fault of my own.

# CHAPTER ELEVEN

# HUDDLE UP

>> If all I had going for me was the game, getting benched might have devastated me. But because I had Leah, football wasn't the most important thing in the world to me. *She* was. Having her in my life made the bad stuff not that bad. Having her in my life made me grateful for what I had instead of angry about what I didn't.

I was feeling so grateful that even though I was benched, I decided to do something to celebrate being in the NFL. Not throw myself another party or something for me, but something that would give back to my hometown. I thought way back to the first time I'd landed in the hospital with my leg injury in high school. I thought about all the kids who were stuck in the hospital at Christmastime. And I decided to be like one of Santa's Helpers that year.

I contacted the folks at A. I. duPont Hospital, where I got my first leg surgery, and I asked if I could come in and give gifts to the children there just before Christmas. Then I went out to Toys "R" Us and bought a few thousand dollars' worth of toys, all out of my own pocket. I put all those toys underneath a tree in one of the rooms there, and then I invited all the kids who were there through the holidays to come pick out any toy they wanted. It was so cool to see all those kids smile. No matter what they were going through, they smiled that day. It was beautiful.

There were some kids who couldn't come down to the room, so I went to them. I wound up hugging kids with cancer and handing presents to these tearful parents who were just so grateful to see their kids light up for a little while.

It was the first time since I'd made it to the NFL that I'd done something really big, really special, for people outside of my own family—and it felt great. It didn't take me long, it didn't take a lot of planning, yet none of those kids or their parents would ever forget it. Neither would I.

I knew then and there that I would always give back, always try to put a smile on other people's faces, always try to help kids and their families who were in pain and going through things that I was lucky enough to not go through myself. Giving back just needed to be a part of my life now.

When the season was over, I decided not to waste any of my NFL money on a new apartment and instead went back to live with my dad in Delaware. His place was cramped, and it was definitely in the hood, but other than the fact that he kept playing old-school K-Ci & JoJo on his stereo, it was fine for me. It was convenient to everywhere I needed to be—not far from my daughter and not far from Asha.

Asha and I started spending all our free time together. I mean *all* of it. I wouldn't have had time to date anybody else if I wanted to—and I didn't want to. She and I were great together. It's like we were the same person.

I think the idea of dating a man with a young daughter would be scary to some women, but Asha took to it like it was the most natural thing in the world. Leah wasn't real nice to her in the beginning.

I think she felt threatened or something, and she put her through some tests. But it didn't take too long before Asha and Leah started getting along like sisters or something, and all three of us spent our days laughing and having fun.

It felt good to be able to buy things for my little girl. Like I said, I didn't have a lot of toys as a kid, so I overdid it just a little bit. On her third birthday, I bought Leah an Audi. Not a real Audi. A little pink plastic princess Audi that was battery powered, so she could drive around the parking lot looking like the princess she was.

I don't know what it was about that first off-season of having Leah in my life full time and having Asha, too, but I just wanted to spread love everywhere I went. I remember when Asha and I went to the mall at Christmastime, I noticed this woman and her kids, and she was clearly struggling. I could tell she was a hardworking single mom the moment I laid eyes on her. She was in this one store, looking at this nice purse, and she clearly thought that bag was beautiful. She just loved it. But she looked at the price tag and then looked at her kids, and she put the bag back. I could tell she was disappointed, but she knew her priorities. She made that choice to not spend money on herself, because she *had* to.

I got it. I knew it. I lived it.

So when she left, I went over and purchased that bag, and then Asha and I went walking through the mall until we found her. Asha gave it to her. "We noticed you admiring this in the store, and we wanted you to have it," we said. She stopped and looked at us for a minute like we were kidding. Then she smiled and was overjoyed. She thanked us again and again.

She turned to Asha and said, "You've got a good man there, girl, you better hold onto him!" and Asha said, "Yeah. I do. I will!"

Sharing the spirit and desire to give to others brought me and Asha closer than ever.

· · ·

By this time in my career, I had kids coming up to me all the time asking for autographs and selfies, and I always asked them what they wanted to do with their lives. Some of them said they wanted to play football, but a lot of them said they weren't sure, so I'd always tell them, "That's okay. Just keep trying. Find what you love. Find what you're good at and do that, and don't give up. Things are going to get in your way. There are going to be obstacles. But don't give up. Work harder, and if something gets in your way, just climb on over it. Make the promise to yourself that you're going to make it happen no matter who or what gets in your way."

After all the ups and downs I'd gone through on my way to the NFL, I hoped those words would serve as a shortcut to those kids—a little inspiration to keep them from doubting themselves in the tough times. Because tough times are inevitable.

My second season in Cincinnati started off great. The tackle who took my spot in the middle of the last season was let go, and I stepped onto the active roster full time—and feeling healthy. We lost our first game of the season. We were still working the kinks out. But then we came together as a team and everything started to click into place. We beat the Steelers and the Packers, then suffered a setback with one really off game where we got trounced by the Cleveland Browns; but we came back the next week and ran all over Tom Brady and the New England Patriots. The next week we beat the Bills in overtime. It started to sink in that this team had a real shot at making the playoffs. There was some serious talk that maybe we had what it took to go all the way to the Super Bowl that year.

I wasn't just playing in the NFL. I was playing for the best team in the AFC North Division.

The next week we headed to Detroit to play the Lions, and I was pumped. I had a great game right from the start. My mind was clear. I was focused. I saw opportunities to make plays everywhere.

One play, I went to tackle Reggie Bush, and when I stuck my

arm out to get him, a linebacker came sprinting up out of nowhere and hit the back of my arm. I felt my elbow pop. I fell to the ground.

I didn't know what had happened; all I heard was turf in my ear and I felt a weird feeling in my arm. I didn't want to stay on the ground, though. I didn't want people to see me like that. So I got right back up, and I was walking to the sideline, and I could feel my arm dangling, and my defensive line coach looked at me and his eyes got all wide, and he said, "Oh my God, somebody—his elbow. His elbow!"

They sat me on a bench and a doctor popped my arm back in place, then took me back to get X-rays. I kept praying that it was just a dream, like, this really didn't happen. But sure enough, they said I dislocated my elbow and it would be six to eight weeks until I got back on the field.

I realized quickly I couldn't do this alone. With a dislocated elbow, I couldn't so much as zip my own pants or tie my own shoes. I couldn't bathe myself. I needed help. I called Asha and she dropped everything to get on a plane and come be with me in Cincinnati. I didn't buy her airline ticket or anything. She paid for it herself. To me, that proved even more how much she cared about me. She wanted to be there for me at any cost, and that meant the world to me. She stayed and helped me with everything. Everything. And she didn't seem put out by it at all. She wanted to see me get better, and she wasn't asking anything in return. She was a natural caretaker. This woman had been caring for her grandmother who'd gone through cancer. Her grandma who'd taken her to church her whole life. Her grandma with the giving heart, who taught her to be kind and have a giving heart too.

I don't mean to get all soft and mushy now, but Asha was like some kind of angel.

I used to ask her sometimes, "Where did you come from?"

"You know where I come from," she'd whisper to me, "'cause you come from the very same place."

I felt strong enough during our bye week to get back home to see Leah and my parents for Thanksgiving, and I was so full of gratitude for Asha and Leah and all of the blessings in my life that I decided I ought to do something about it. I decided I wanted to give something back in return. It was cold that week. Blistering cold. And when I drove by the Mission, the local homeless shelter, I thought about all those people from my hometown who must've been hurting something fierce in those cold temperatures. So, I turned the car around and headed to Burlington Coat Factory. Asha and I grabbed a couple of shopping carts, and we went to the racks and started stuffing those carts full of warm winter coats. We picked out the best ones we could find, from North Face and Patagonia—like, the warmest ones, in all different sizes.

"How many you want to get?" Asha asked.

"Let's do seventy-five, for my number: 75!" I said. And we just kept piling them up.

We checked out and drove straight to the shelter and started handing out those seventy-five coats, and everyone was so grateful and smiling you would've thought the Pope had just stopped by to bless them all in person or something. It was beautiful. It felt amazing. But more than that, it was the right thing to do. I had enough money to buy coats for all those people who needed them. What kind of a man would I be if I didn't spend that money and do that for those people?

I swear that turned out to be the best Thanksgiving ever. I'd never really recognized it before, but Thanksgiving isn't just about being thankful for what we have; Thanksgiving is also about being thankful for what we have to *give*.

Back in Cincinnati, with Asha there to help me and after having been through so many injuries before, I found I was able to push myself a little bit harder than the average football player. I ended up coming back from that injury in just five weeks. I got back on the active roster for our wins over San Diego and Indianapolis the next two weeks and was pumped to go all-in against the Steelers on December 15. It was cold that day, and Heinz stadium is right on the river. So I was freezing cold. I wished I could've worn one of those North Face jackets on the field. I was really uncomfortable. It felt like the cold was affecting my muscles, but I pushed through it.

I shouldn't have.

During one play I tried to lock somebody out—and I felt a pop in my back. A pop like the ones I'd experienced in the past.

When we got back to Cincinnati that day, I told one of the trainers, "I'm gonna need one of those shots again because I can't even walk." They set me up to get the shot the next day, only this time, it didn't work. The pain didn't go away. I told them I didn't want to get put on IR because the team was going to the playoffs. I wanted to play in the NFL playoffs for the first time! I was willing to take the pain to get to that whole new pinnacle in my career and to do my part to help us win. But they told me to rest up and see how I felt in a couple of days.

I told my coach I really wanted to play in that game, so he took me out on the field before it started and said, "If you can come out of your stance and run, I'll put you in."

We walked out to the field, and he went to say "hi" to another coach. When he did, I decided to do a practice run. As soon as I popped up, I felt a sharp feeling go down my leg. My foot went numb. As I walked off the field, he looked at me and said, "What happened?"

"I can't do it," I said. "I can't play."

I asked Asha if she would fly out to Cincinnati again. She did. She saw firsthand how much pain I was in, but I kept fighting it. I couldn't sleep because of it. I would try to sleep on all fours, or I'd go into the living room and lay on the floor and put my leg up on the couch because I couldn't deal with the pain. It got so bad one day, Asha made me go to the emergency room, and they basically told me that I was going to have to get surgery. I didn't have a choice. So, I went back and told the trainers, "You're gonna have to put me on IR. I can't do this anymore."

I ended up getting that surgery, and I started on my road to recovery. I wanted to do my rehab back home in Delaware so I could be close to Leah during my downtime. About a week after I got the surgery, I flew home. My dad's apartment was too small for the three of us to come there, so we stayed in a hotel. I had to wear a back brace, and I was wearing it kind of tight, just so I could have a lot of support for my back. One morning right after Asha went to work, I felt a pain in my rib area. I didn't know what it was, so I loosened up my brace thinking maybe I had it too tight.

I ended up calling my dad, and I went over to his house. Walking to the door, I had the sharpest pain in my ribs. It was so sharp that I just laid down right there on the ground. The pain kept getting worse and worse, and I started crying. My dad was like, "What's wrong with you?" I told him the pain I was having, and he said, "Let's go the hospital." I refused. I wanted to believe that I was recovering. This wasn't a setback. "No, I'm not going to the hospital. I'll be good, just let me sleep this off."

Five minutes later when I was still moaning in pain, he said, "Now I'm not asking you. I'm telling you. We're going."

That hospital was busy. They left me on a bed in the hallway for like two hours. I kept telling my dad I wanted to go home, but he insisted I stay put.

I'm glad he did.

They finally ran an EKG and an ultrasound on me, and they found three blood clots in my lungs.

"You're lucky you came in when you did," the doctor told me. "If you'd waited another day, you probably wouldn't have made it."

"You mean I might be dead?" I said.

"Yes," the doctor said.

We got some other doctors involved, and they came up with a

treatment plan, and I thought this was just like any other injury I'd ever overcome. It might take time, but I'd get through it.

But then one of the doctors said something I could not believe.

"Devon, I'm sorry if this hasn't been made clear to you, but with this condition—you're not going to be able to play football again."

• • •

I was lost. I didn't know what to do. My mother kept crying. My dad was upset. I couldn't even face Leah. Why was all of this happening? Why was my body failing me? Why was everything falling apart?

If it weren't for the strength of Asha's arms holding me after the doctors gave me that news, I'm not sure what I would have done. They might as well have told me that my whole life was over. Without football, what did I have? I had nothing. I had no career. The money would be gone. My parents would go right back to struggling. Leah's future would be gone.

"Devon, stop," Asha said. "First of all, I don't believe those doctors. They don't know you. They don't know what you're capable of. I've seen you come back stronger and faster than anyone else thought you could."

"But why does this keep happening? Why do I keep getting shot down? Why does my body keep breaking? Why does everything keep going wrong just when it starts to go right?"

"Maybe because we don't have a relationship with God, Devon," she said.

Her words stopped me cold.

"You're absolutely right," she said. "Things do keep going wrong. Again and again. Maybe God's trying to tell us something. Maybe we need to change. Maybe we need to stop ignoring the signs and get ourselves to church and try to find a relationship with God. That's what my grandma always told me. We don't have the answers. We don't know everything. We need to get to church and get answers from God."

I was silent. I didn't expect to hear all that. I hadn't thought of God at all, not through any of this. I wasn't even praying now and then like I used to at Penn State. It wasn't on purpose. I didn't purposefully turn my back on God or nothing like that. I'd just let God slip out of my life.

"You know, when I got in trouble when I was a kid, my grandma dragged me to church too," I said.

"And what happened after that?"

"I didn't pay much attention. I just went through the motions, you know?"

"Yeah, but what happened after? Did things change?"

"I. . . ."

I thought about it, and the only answer I could come up with was yes. I'd never given any credit to the church for helping me turn my life around, but it was only *after* grandma dragged me to church and put me in the church choir and everything else that my life finally turned around. It was *after* that when my dad got the notion to throw me in jail to try to scare me straight. It was *after* that when I stopped stealing and started living right.

"I guess things got better," I said. "I don't know. Things are so bad right now, I'd be willing to try almost anything. I can't lose football, Asha. I can't."

"Then let's go get some help."

The two of us reached out to our mutual friend, John, whose faith had only grown deeper since he turned his life around after getting thrown from a car. He was downright excited to hear from us. I told him Asha was the one who suggested we call, and he said, "Aw, Devon. You got yourself a good woman there. You better hold on to her."

I looked at Asha and said, "I know."

He recommended we come down to his church that Sunday

where he was leading Bible studies and working as a youth minister. This church was real small, a white stucco building with stained glass and old wooden pews inside; the kind of place where they have to put fans in the windows when it's hot outside, because the air conditioners don't work, and when the old steam heat kicks on it clanks and hisses through the metal radiators.

We weren't sure what to expect, and we weren't real comfortable in that church at first, because when the Pentecostals pray, they pray hard. I'm talking crying and walking all around with their hands up in the air, wailing and weeping and shouting. We weren't sure what to make of it. But we listened. We took it all in. We read the Bible. We sang. I wasn't real open, just because I wasn't used to it, but I tried to let the spirit of Christ and the welcoming arms of that little church take me in. I had nothing to lose except everything, so I gave it my full attention and just tried to go along with the idea that this was all meant to be. We were meant to be there. We'd been lead there by our circumstances, and the friends we shared who had been through so much in their lives.

Even though I was reluctant, I put my heart into it. I listened to the words of the preacher, words I didn't bother listening to when I was younger. I read passages that I didn't bother reading when I was a kid. I heard the words of the songs in those hymns, and I prayed every night—for guidance, for love, for my daughter, for Asha, for myself, for my parents, for Charlie, for John, for all of my friends, for all of our health, for peace, for understanding. I just kept praying. I tried to give myself over to God in every way I could think of, and I put it all in His hands. There was nothing else I could do. The doctors had done all they could. I'd given all I had to give. There was no other medicine I could take, no other workout I could do. I truly had nowhere else to turn but to God.

We tried to get life back to normal after that, as best we could. We enrolled Leah in a preschool dance and gymnastics class, and she thought learning ballet and hip-hop and all kinds of tumbles and things was the greatest thing on earth. Her class was on Tuesday, and every day of the week she'd wake up and the first thing she'd ask us was, "Is it Tuesday today?"

I invited her mom to come watch her in those classes, and on most weeks, she came. So Leah could look up from the mat and out through the window and see both her mom and her dad sitting there watching her and smiling. I didn't know if we'd be able to keep up that routine of showing up together her whole life like my parents had. Her mom and I definitely had tension between us every time we were in the same room together. But for the time being, it was working. And I knew how much those little moments of seeing us together and supporting her would mean to Leah because I'd experienced it myself, firsthand.

One Sunday, about a month after we started to go to church, I remember the pastor saying, "Something really big is going to happen to somebody this week," and I prayed that he was talking about me. He couldn't have known this, but that upcoming Wednesday I had an appointment to meet with the doctors to determine whether the medications they put me on for my blood clots had been working. It was basically my last chance to give some kind of good news to the Bengals, or I would be in serious danger of getting cut from the team.

Sure enough, we went to see the doctors on Wednesday, and they told me that every blood clot was gone. Every one of them. More than that, they saw absolutely no residue, nothing to indicate that I would clot up again. It appeared the underlying condition that caused those clots in the first place had up and disappeared.

It was, in my mind and in Asha's mind, nothing short of a miracle. And we were certain it had happened because we had let God into our lives.

"So, does this mean . . . ?"

"Yeah. I see no reason why you can't get back on the football field," the lead doctor said.

*Praise God.* Asha and I cried tears of joy. I was cleared to play football again, and we were sure it was because we were on the right path.

I went back out to Cincinnati the next week and started rehabbing my back. That went well too. Miraculously well. One day I was training with one of our trainers, Nick, and when I was going through drills, he was like, "Devon, you have some of the best feet that I've seen out there, even better than the skilled players. I can't wait to see you play this year. And you're finally healthy, with nothing holding you back!"

I was excited. To get praised like that by Nick, someone who sees a lot of NFL athletes training—that really meant something.

I was starting to believe more and more that everything, truly *everything*, was on the right path.

Things were so good it felt like we ought to be celebrating. So that April of 2014, I decided to take us on a trip to Disney World. We flew down to Orlando. After we got on a shuttle bus from the airport to the hotel, I had my girlfriend and my daughter sitting in front of me, and I just started crying, thinking, *My daughter's about to experience something that I never experienced before. Like, we're about to create memories that will last forever, all because I never gave up. All thanks to God.*

We had the time of our lives. All three of us were like little kids. They even got me to wear mouse ears. In public. And put it on Instagram. There were no other girls besides Asha and Leah in the whole wide world who could've convinced me to do that in public!

Leah loved the little Snow White roller coaster–type ride. We went on it a bunch of times, and every time she laughed at the Seven Dwarfs, gasped at the crazy parts, and got all serious at the sight of the evil witch. I loved how much she paid attention to everything all the time. Her favorite ride of all though was "It's a Small World." She made us go on it again and again and again. She sang that song every day we were there.

We went morning 'til night, four days straight, staying all the way through the magic of the fireworks before heading back to the hotel to collapse into our beds. And there was only one time when Leah slowed down. It was real strange. We were walking down one of those crazy busy streets in the middle of the park, and she just stopped. She sat down on the pavement, right in the middle of the street, and wouldn't budge.

"Leah, what are you doing?" I asked her. It was embarrassing.

"My legs hurt. I don't want to move," she said.

"Leah, come on now. You can't just sit on the ground in the middle of all these people! What are you doing? We got to go!"

But she wouldn't move.

She'd taken to throwing these little tantrums now and then, or saying that her hip hurt. I was sure it was just all the hard work she was putting into her gymnastics and dance classes. But she only ever seemed to complain when we were asking her to go clean her room or something. We were at Disney. She loved this! I could not understand why she wouldn't get up.

I wondered if this was her tiny, cute version of the terrible twos coming a year late or something.

My mother even made a few comments about it when we were back home, how Leah would complain about hurting and wouldn't want to move.

"Girl, there is nothing wrong with you. Now come on and help me clear the table," she'd say.

Eventually, Leah always got up, just like she finally got up at Disney World that day and got back to having fun. But it was frustrating. I suppose it was nothing much compared to some of the bad behaviors we saw from some other kids at Disney World, though. It's amazing to see the size of the temper tantrums that unfold in the happiest place on earth. I just laughed it off. At her worst, Leah was just about the smiliest, most beautiful little kid anyone could ever hope for. If those little frustrations were all we had to worry about, we were lucky. And I knew it.

Asha and I felt so lucky and so blessed about everything when we came back from that trip that we decided to do something big. We decided to get baptized. I had never been baptized. Asha had been baptized, but it was when she was a baby. It wasn't her choice back then. Now? We wanted to get baptized together in the church that had already brought us one miracle and had helped to set our lives on a better path.

So that April, we got baptized. In the name of the Father, the Son, and the Holy Spirit, we committed ourselves to God.

Everything felt right with the world.

# CHAPTER TWELVE

# BLINDSIDED

>> Back in Cincinnati, my rehab was going so well that I didn't hesitate to ask if I could skip a few days.

"My daughter's got a dance recital back in Delaware," I told my coach. "I really want to be there. I want her to look up and know that her dad's there supporting her, you know?"

"Yeah, go ahead," he said. "Your rehab is going well and you're on the right path. So that won't be a problem."

I flew back for the weekend, and I watched Leah practice her dance moves at Asha's apartment, seemingly happy and healthy as could be. Her grandmother picked her up for the night on Sunday and on Monday morning, June 2, she took her out to breakfast.

Right after I dropped Asha off at her job at Zales jewelers, my cell phone rang.

"Leah's not feeling good," her grandma said. "She has a fever and she's not eating any of her food. You should call her pediatrician and set up an appointment for her."

"Where are you?" I asked.

"We're at IHOP."

Leah loves IHOP. Is there any kid in America who doesn't flip for the International House of Pancakes? For my four-year-old daughter to be there with her grandmother and not eating was surely a sign that Leah must be really sick.

Funny thing was, just as Leah's grandmother was giving me that news, I came to a stop at the intersection almost directly across from that very IHOP. On any other day, I might not have dropped Asha off at the mall in the morning and would not have wound up in that exact spot. If I hadn't been so close, I might have continued on my way, called the pediatrician, and left Leah in the good care of her grandmother. But on this day, something told me to stop and see what was going on.

I had learned to follow my gut.

So, I turned the car left at the light and then into the parking lot, and inside the restaurant I found Leah with her head down on her forearms on the table. She didn't even look up when she heard my voice. That wasn't like her. I sat down next to her and asked her if she was okay, and she just shook her head and wouldn't speak to me.

"How long she been like this?" I asked.

"Almost the whole time we've been here. I really think she ought to go see a doctor, maybe right away if you can get her in."

I thanked her for calling me, and I picked Leah up and carried her to the car. She was still so little, but she seemed heavier that day. Her body just sort of flopped up onto my shoulder. She seemed weak, too, like she could barely lift her arms around my neck. I could feel that she had a fever as soon as her forehead touched my skin, and I knew this had to be something serious. A bad flu. Pneumonia, maybe. The type of thing that really wipes a kid out.

I noticed there was an urgent care clinic right down the street. I'd never been there before, and I didn't know if they took our insurance or anything, but not wanting to waste any time, I drove directly there and parked the car again. It seemed like a nice enough place, and I was real hopeful they'd be able to give her some medicine to make her feel better, because her dance recital was that night. She'd been looking forward to it for a very long time, and I'd flown all the way back from Cincinnati just to see her dance. After we'd been there for a while, though, and after they had run a few tests, the doctors and nurses said they weren't sure what was going on. There didn't seem to be any sort of infection, and her lungs seemed clear, so it wasn't pneumonia or anything obvious that would cause that sort of fever and fatigue.

They asked me whether I'd noticed anything else wrong with her in the days before that morning, and I told them the only thing I could think of: "She has been complaining about some hip pain," I said. I thought her aches came from being into gymnastics and falling off the balance beams and stuff like that. I told them I didn't think it was anything serious, because she only seemed to complain about it when we told her to clean her room. Like, as soon as we would say, "Leah, go clean your room," she would grab her leg and say, "Oh, my hip!" We truly didn't think much of it.

That's when the doctor pressed on Leah's hip to examine it and my little girl jumped away from him like she'd been stuck by a cattle prod. Just the speed of her motion in that lethargic state told me how much that hip must've been hurting her.

The doctor said something about there being a possible infection in her hip, something that can happen when kids grow too fast. Since I wasn't exactly the shortest guy in the room, I thought that sounded like a real possibility. Maybe my little Leah was starting to sprout up.

That clinic had done all it could at that point, so they sent us over to A.I. duPont Hospital, which was only a few minutes from where we were standing. Once we were there, we had to go over everything again, and I told them everything the doctors at the clinic had mentioned. At that point, they decided to go ahead and do some more blood work.

Leah was so out of it, she didn't even put up a fight about the needle. She just sat there, her tiny arm flopped out in the nurse's hand. I had to look away as she filled those vials with my little girl's blood. I kept thinking, *Isn't this just a flu or something? Why can't they just give her some antibiotics and send her home so she can rest up and feel better?*

I called Leah's mother at that point. I figured she ought to know what was going on. I knew it would be awkward to sit side by side, because things were uncomfortable between us. But she's her mom, and my little girl needed her mother.

Leah slept on the hospital bed as I waited for the results of the blood work to come in, and finally after about an hour, the doctor came into the room and told me Leah could be suffering from any of ten different things. The last thing he mentioned on that list was "cancer," and because "cancer" was the last thing he said, I didn't pay much attention to it. I figured that word was just a far-out, worst-case scenario kind of thing that they mentioned to cover themselves, you know? If cancer or something that serious was a real possibility, they certainly would have mentioned it a lot higher up on the list, right?

As we lay in that hospital bed together, I snapped a selfie of the two of us like I would have on any normal day. Leah lit up and smiled for the photo. She loved Instagram. Still in a daze from this whole turn of events, I typed the message, "Crazy how everything can be good one minute but the next everything can change been in the hospital all day but no matter what I have faith in my God that everything's gonna be ok so we gonna continue to smile through the bs."

I left out details. I truly thought this was going to turn out to be some kind of infection in her hip. But I believed in the power of prayer, and I wanted as many prayers as possible to get sent up to God for my daughter.

>> ME AND MY BROTHER AND OUR
DOG, MARIO, AT HOME IN CAMDEN

ME BACK AT OUR HOUSE
ON KYNLYN DRIVE
⌃

>> HAPPY BIRTHDAY
WITH MOM AND DAD

ME WITH MY <<
BROTHER AND
MY SISTER,
SHAQUARA

LOOKING SHARP AT MY
PARENTS' WEDDING »

» PICTURE DAY
WITH DAD, AFTER
WE'D MOVED TO
CLAYMONT

US THREE KIDS ON A FAMILY TRIP  «
TO SIX FLAGS, JUST AFTER WE
MOVED BACK IN WITH OUR DAD

MY LITTLE LEAGUE
FOOTBALL TEAM,
THE RAIDERS. THAT'S  «
ME ON THE FAR LEFT
WITH THE OTHER
TEAM CAPTAINS.

>> HIGH SCHOOL FOOTBALL–MY SENIOR YEAR

MAKING MOM PROUD ON NATIONAL SIGNING DAY–I WAS HEADED TO PENN STATE! <<

>> EARLY ADVERSITY

SIGNING MY FIRST << AUTOGRAPH AT PENN STATE

>> ME AND COACH PATERNO
WALKING BACK INTO THE
TUNNEL AFTER ONE OF HIS
LAST GAMES

FEEDING MY
LITTLE GIRL FOR <<
THE FIRST TIME

>> BABY LEAH–SMILING
FROM THE START

MY LITTLEST FAN <<

>> DRESSED TO IMPRESS ON EASTER SUNDAY

PASSING OUT CHRISTMAS GIFTS AT THE SAME HOSPITAL LEAH WOULD GET DIAGNOSED AT A YEAR LATER << 

>> MY TWO GIRLS ON OUR FIRST TRIP TO DISNEY

LONG NIGHTS ON A COT WERE TOUGH ON MY BACK, AND THE EARLY TREATMENTS WERE TOUGH ON EVERYONE. << 

>> WATCHING MOVIES
TO PASS THE TIME

CELEBRATING
CHRISTMAS IN STYLE <<

LEAH STRONG! SPEAKING
THE MESSAGE OF HER
T-SHIRT INTO EXISTENCE

I STILL THANK GOD FOR ASHA. <<

>> WE KNEW RIGHT AWAY
WE WERE MEANT FOR
EACH OTHER.

ON THE RED CARPET
AT THE ESPYS RIGHT <<
BEFORE MY SPEECH

>> READY FOR SOME
TRICK-OR-TREATING

BEST FEELING IN THE WORLD,
SHOWING LEAH MY ALL <<
AMERICAN PLAQUE AT PSU

ONE OF THE BEST DAYS
OF MY LIFE

KISSING THE BRIDE

LEAH GIVING
HER SPEECH
AT THE
RECEPTION

BLESSED

To try to get to the bottom of it, the doctors decided to have Leah sit for an ultrasound of her abdomen and hip. I was thankful she was so sleepy that she wouldn't worry about all of this stuff she was going through. She didn't want to leave my side, and I sat right there holding her little hand in mine as they squeezed the cool gel onto her abdomen and started pressing that machine on her belly. I told her it was going to be okay, and I truly believed that. I was sure it was just a bug of some kind.

That's when the technician saw a mass in Leah's stomach—and my stomach just about sank through the floor. A doctor came in to see for himself and said they couldn't be sure what it was, but they wanted to run some more tests immediately. They decided to send her up for an MRI and a CAT scan, and that's when I made some more phone calls. Leah's grandmother was out in the waiting room, and I told her what was happening. I called Asha, but she couldn't leave work. There was no one to cover for her. I called my parents, and my dad came right down.

"Don't worry," I told Leah as they started to wheel my little girl out of the room. "I've had CAT scans with lots of my injuries, and it doesn't hurt, okay? Not at all. You just have to lie there real still and rest, okay?"

"Okay, Daddy," Leah said.

I had never felt more helpless in my life than that moment when I watched a team of people in hospital garb wheel my beautiful child down a fluorescent-lit hallway into the unknown.

From all of the injuries I'd been through in my career, I knew that CAT scans and MRIs usually only take forty-five minutes to an hour. When we hit the two-hour mark in that waiting room, I knew something was seriously wrong.

Finally, a nurse came out and told us that the doctor would be in with the results soon. Leah's mom had arrived by then, so they asked us both to step away from the crowded waiting room.

I felt like I was going to throw up.

We sat there in awkward silence.

Ten minutes later the doctor came walking through the back door, and before she said a word I could see her lip start to shake.

"We found a tumor in Leah's stomach," she said. "We believe that it's neuroblastoma, a form of cancer."

And just like that, all the air got sucked out of me. I couldn't breathe. It's like I was asleep at the line of scrimmage, standing there with my eyes closed when a 300-pound lineman came out of nowhere and slammed helmet-first into my ribs. I can't even explain what I was feeling. I don't even know what else was said after I heard that word: *cancer.*

I broke out of my daze just as the doctor said she would go to the waiting room to share the news with Leah's grandparents.

"No," I said. "If they're gonna hear something like this, it has to come from a family member. I don't want a stranger telling them."

"I understand," the doctor said.

I got up and walked to the waiting room, and I saw my dad sitting there with Leah's grandma, and when I went to open my mouth to tell them what happened my whole body went weak. I felt the room spin, and I collapsed. I nearly blacked out. All six feet, five inches of me fell to the ground, and I barely managed to put my arms out to stop my head from smashing into the cold tile floor. I started to cry. My dad came up and knelt down and started rubbing my back.

"What is it?" he kept asking. "Devon?"

I couldn't speak. I couldn't find the words.

Finally I just blurted it out.

"Cancer."

Everyone stopped breathing. There was no more sound. It was like the whole world stopped.

My dad bowed his head in pure sadness like I'd never seen, and out of the corner of my eye, through the blur of my tears, I saw Leah's grandmother drop her purse. Its contents spilled out all over the floor, and she didn't even look after it. I was about to yell, to tell her to sit down, to tell somebody to help her, but she put her hand over her mouth as her eyes welled up and she turned and ran out of the room.

She knew. Somehow all of us knew. In one moment, with one word, our lives were changed forever.

• • •

Leah didn't go to her dance recital that night. It quickly became clear to all of us that she wouldn't be leaving that hospital any-time soon.

I was alone with her in the room when they came to hook her up to an IV. She saw the needles come out, and she started screaming. "Daddy! Why did you bring me here? This is all your fault! This is all your fault! You never should have brought me here!"

She didn't mean it that way. I know she didn't. She blamed being at the hospital as the reason for getting those needles stuck in her. But I still couldn't take it. I had to excuse myself and step out into the hallway, 'cause I burst into tears right then and I didn't want Leah to see me cry.

We all spent that night sleepless in the hospital. Leah didn't know what cancer was. She didn't know what was going on. I told her the doctors had to do some more tests, which was true, but then I just tried to convince her that this was like staying in another hotel.

"You like hotels, don't you?" I asked her.

"I love hotels!" she said. "Is there a pool?"

"No," I said, laughing a little when all I wanted to do was cry. "No pool," I told her.

In the morning, I called the Bengals to let them know what was happening. They told me to stay with my daughter the rest of the week and take the time I needed to sort things out. That same morning, a nurse came in to take Leah for a walk, and she gave her a walker. A little tiny version of one of those metal walkers some old person would use when their legs wore out after a lifetime's use.

"Why does she need that?" I asked.

"Her bones are too brittle to walk without it. We don't want to risk a break," she said.

I'd just watched her dance at Asha's apartment. She'd gone to gymnastics a couple of days before that. She was supposed to do her recital just last night!

*Oh my God*, I thought. *What if all that was hurting her? What about what happened at Disney? My mom's house? Those times when she didn't want to move, when she complained about hurting and didn't want to do her chores. Why didn't I listen? Why didn't we pay more attention? What if we hurt her worse by not listening?*

That afternoon, the initial test results came back and confirmed it was neuroblastoma—but the tests showed cancer wasn't just in the mass in her stomach. The cancer had spread. The tests suggested that my daughter had stage 4 neuroblastoma, the worst kind she could possibly have.

The doctor pulled me and her mom down a long hallway near her room and told us the straight-up truth: "It'll be forty-eight hours before it's 100 percent confirmed, but it looks like stage 4, which means her chances of survival are around 50 percent."

This time, Leah's mom collapsed on the floor.

"Doc, what do we do? What do we do?" I asked.

"Well, you have some decisions to make," the doctor said. He was a white-haired man in khakis, different from the emergency doctor we'd seen the day before. This was a teaching hospital. One of the best children's hospitals in the country. We'd seen all kinds of different doctors and interns, which felt like getting second, third, and fourth opinions all in one place. But it also felt strange, like all these strangers were giving us our fate. "We can start her on chemo right away. But there are options," he said. "There are clinical trials happening at other hospitals. There are options we can't offer you here. So, I think we need to think it through. We'll look into options on our end, and you should feel free to do some research on your own, and we should come to a treatment decision that's best for Leah."

"Don't we need to do something right now? Not wait?" I asked.

"She's been living with this for some time, so no. Waiting a few days won't make a difference in her outcomes at this point. We'll keep her comfortable until the decision is made, and we'll do what's best for your daughter. Okay?"

"Yeah. Okay," I said.

The doctor explained again that there were more tests being done, to determine exactly what kind of cancer it was and to confirm that it was stage 4, and that we wouldn't have results for another two days.

I tried to find something positive in that. I took his words to mean that the tests might possibly confirm that it *wasn't* stage 4. In my mind, I thought, *Maybe those tests will show it's not cancer at all!*

I felt like I couldn't breathe. I needed to pray. And I needed to pray *hard*.

At church, we'd heard about people fasting as a way to get closer to God, so I decided that needed to be my first course of action. I stopped eating.

Leah was asleep, so I took the elevator downstairs and walked through the lobby just to get some air. Toward the other side of the building, I saw a sign for a chapel, and I followed it. The doors were closed but unlocked, so I went in.

It was a small room with light wooden chairs all facing a full-sized wall of stained glass. In that glass were images of lambs and of children, all being cared for by grown-ups, regaining their health, surrounded by flowers and trees like the Garden of Eden. There was a little altar off to one side and a raised area in front of the stained glass, like a little platform stage, where I collapsed to my knees and started praying the kind of prayers I encountered at the Pentecostal church. I'd learned in that church that if you want to feel God's presence, just ask for it. So in the privacy of that room, I let everything out. I started bawling and calling out loud, "Why, God? Why?" I had snot running from my nose as I begged, "Please help us. Please heal her. Please! Take the cancer out of her and put it into me. I beg you. Please. Are you here with me, God? Do you hear me? Let me know that you're here!"

All of a sudden, the doors to the chapel started rattling. There were doors on both sides, and all of 'em were rattling, as if there were people out there pulling on those doors, trying to get in. But those doors don't lock. I knew that because I'd just come through them. The hair on my arms stood up straight. I got scared.

I stood up. The rattling stopped. I wiped the snot and tears from my face, and I walked back out into the hallway. There was no one there. I checked the news to make sure there hadn't been an earthquake or some other crazy coincidence, and there wasn't. There was nothing. There was only one explanation: all that rattling was God trying to let me know He was there.

That night, I climbed into Leah's hospital bed and fell asleep right next to her.

Around midnight something woke me up.

Leah was wide awake and pressing her hands into my stomach.

"What are you doing, Leah?" I whispered.

I looked down and she scooped her hands over the surface of her stomach, like she was digging in a sandbox or something, and then she pressed what she'd scooped up into my midsection.

"Leah?"

"I'm taking the cancer out of me and giving it to you," she whispered.

I was astonished. Had God heard my prayer?

• • •

I went two days without eating in a state of near-constant prayer, asking God to let her test results come back with no sign of cancer. I didn't care one bit if that cancer was in me. I just wanted my daughter to be well.

Each morning a group of eight to ten doctors and interns came in and examined our little girl, and then stepped into the hallway to discuss their findings with us. I couldn't comprehend most of what they were saying. It's like they were speaking a foreign language. I realized that, in addition to prayer, I also needed to get educated.

There was a computer at a desk across the hall from Leah's room, and I sat there for hours, Googling neuroblastoma and various pediatric cancers and treatments, unlocking a door to a world of pain and sadness I had never seen before. On the one hand, it helped. It's like I took a crash course in the terminology of my daughter's disease, even while praying she didn't really have it. But on the other, I read story after story of children's final words and final days, tributes from grieving parents, conflicting medical studies and reports, and statistics that made it seem like kids who were diagnosed had little chance of long-term survival. Even kids who beat their cancer saw it come back, again and again, until it took them once and for all. It was agonizing.

"Devon, you've got to eat something," my dad said. "You look worn out."

"No, no. I need to fast," I argued. "I need to."

"Please, Devon," my mother said. "What you need is to be strong for your daughter."

I couldn't take it. I didn't want anyone telling me what to do. I didn't want to be there. I didn't want my daughter in that hospital. I wanted all of this to go away!

I turned away and went downstairs again. I wandered aimlessly, catching my reflection in the windows to an outdoor courtyard and feeling like I was trapped inside. I just wanted out.

The hallways were painted every shade of the rainbow in that hospital. It was beautiful. It felt like a place where kids should go to have fun, not get diagnosed with cancer.

God was there. Clearly God was in that building.

I just hoped He'd take care of my Leah.

When I went back upstairs, the doctor was looking for me. He had the test results back. My prayers had failed. It was definitely stage 4 neuroblastoma.

I was shattered. But I also knew this wasn't the time for me to fall down. Leah didn't need any tears from me. She needed my strength.

She had slept a lot those first couple of days, but when I walked back into her room she was wide awake, and she wanted to know what was going on.

"Why am I still here?" she asked me.

"Leah," I said. "You have cancer. It's a disease, and the doctors are keeping you here just to try to make sure you're strong enough to fight it."

"Well, how long is that gonna take?" she asked in that tiny voice of hers.

"I don't know," I said. "I don't know. It's gonna be a big fight though. So you're just gonna have to take it round by round."

I didn't have the heart to tell her what her chances were. What good would that have done? I think a lot of adults hear the word cancer and immediately think they're going to die, so a part of them gives up fighting right then and there. There was no way I was going to let my little girl have even one thought about dying. Not yet. Not now. All she needed to know is that she needed to get strong, and she needed to fight.

"You know, it's just like when I hurt my back, or when I dislocated my elbow, I had to fight to get back in the game, right?" I said.

"Yeah," Leah responded.

"It took some time. It took some work. I had to be patient. I had to be strong. But I got back in the game, didn't I?"

"Yeah," Leah said.

"And that's what you gotta do too. Alright?"

"Alllll-right," she said.

Once she agreed, I knew it was game time. I believed she was strong enough to fight this.

Leah was so tired, though, we wound up keeping her at A.I. duPont until we decided on a course of treatment. It felt like that took a month. In actuality, it was another seven days.

I stayed right there at the hospital every one of those days, talking to doctors, doing research. I didn't want to leave her side. In fact, I contemplated quitting football altogether. I was willing to give up my dream so I wouldn't have to leave my daughter's side, until somebody pointed out that the only reason Leah was in that hospital and could even think about receiving the kind of care we wanted was because of the insurance I had through the NFL.

"How much does cancer treatment cost?" I asked.

"The whole thing?" they said.

"Yeah, altogether. I mean—"

"Oh, my goodness. Well over a million dollars by the time everything's said and done."

My heart nearly stopped. I knew I was lucky. I knew I was like one in a million getting into the NFL. I was making good money. But I didn't have a million dollars in the bank, and there was definitely no way that I'd have any way of making a million dollars if I quit the NFL!

"It's okay because of your insurance," they told me. "It will cover the costs 100 percent."

Without that insurance, what might have happened?

I hadn't even thought about that aspect of it, and all of a sudden I started thinking about all of the other families in that hospital, and in hospitals all over the country. How do people do this? In all the talk of cancer I'd heard in my life, no one had ever told me how much it costs. This hospital stay alone was costing thousands of dollars per day. If I didn't have football, we wouldn't have been there. And I got this really bad feeling that if I didn't have football in the future, my daughter might not have a shot at getting through this. Which made me think back to everything that had happened, and the miracle God made in getting rid of my blood clots and getting me back on the field.

It suddenly occurred to me that maybe those miracles weren't even about me. Maybe those miracles were for Leah.

The Bengals were totally understanding. They gave me as much leeway as they could. They basically gave me a free pass to do what I needed to do to take care of my family. "Football will be here," they said. As long as I made it back for training camp in late July, everything would work out fine, they said.

That meant Leah had me or someone else from our family with her at all hours of every day, and I know that helped keep her spirits up. I kept reminding her this was just like being in a hotel. We started doing puzzles and playing games together and watching TV shows together, as if we were on vacation. We tried to make the most of every day.

We could have started her on chemotherapy right there at A.I. duPont, but I was dead set against letting anyone put anything in my daughter's body until we knew we were doing the best thing possible. And it turned out that the best thing possible, the most cutting-edge treatment out there, something called MIBG, was only happening at one of two hospitals in the country: the Children's Hospital of Philadelphia (or CHoP, as most people call it), and Cincinnati Children's Hospital.

Cincinnati! Of all places in the country, the number-one success rate for treating pediatric neuroblastoma like Leah's was in Bengals territory!

We put a plan into action. To get Leah started as soon as possible, we would transport her to CHoP and get the MIBG treatment underway. Then, as soon as we could get things settled, we would move Leah up to Cincinnati so I'd be able to continue my work, keep our insurance, and also be able to see my daughter.

Asha was all ready to come live with me full time anyway, so she'd be there to help out. And I agreed I'd get Leah's mom an apartment there too.

She was hesitant about that.

"Look, it's not forever. It's just temporary. It's for Leah. I'll pay for everything. You know it's the best thing for her if we both can be there supporting her as much as possible. My football career is what's providing her insurance. This allows me to do that, and to be there with her. *And* it's the hospital with the best record for curing this type of cancer!"

Her own mother even volunteered to move to Cincinnati with her, so she'd have additional support. At that point Leah's mom nodded her head and agreed, so I went to work making all the arrangements.

Before Leah left for CHoP, Leah's doctors broke the news to her that she was going to lose her hair because of the chemo. She wasn't happy about that. Not at all.

So I decided to do something to make her less anxious about it. I snuck away from the hospital for a couple of hours and went back to my childhood barber in Wilmington. I asked him to shave my head.

I came back to the hospital wearing a Polo baseball cap, so she wouldn't notice right away. I lay down in bed next to her. Then I took the hat off.

"Daddy! You're bald!" she said, and she started rubbing my head.

"This way, when you lose your hair, we'll be twins," I said.

She kept rubbing my head and laughing. I liked my hair too! I never imagined I'd shave my head in my life. For anyone. But it was worth it. It was worth it just to see my daughter smile.

Leah got scared again the next day when the men came in with a stretcher to load her up into the ambulance for the big move to CHoP. "Baby! It's okay," I said as she clung onto my neck. "We're just gonna go for a fun ride, and they're gonna let you watch princess movies in the ambulance. How many kids get to ride in an ambulance like this? You're one of the lucky ones!" I told her.

Everything's about perspective, right?

Princess movies and the thought of a fun ride was all it took. Leah relaxed, and we climbed into that ambulance together and turned on the DVD player, and she smiled the whole forty-five-minute ride to Philadelphia.

CHoP is a giant place. It's like skyscrapers in a downtown area, right alongside the highway, with different wings on different blocks. It's a modern-looking glass-front building with all kinds of colored lights and an incredible open lobby that stretches six stories into the air, topped by a roof full of skylights with a giant, abstract mobile hanging from the ceiling. This hospital has its own radio station that broadcasts to all the rooms, paid for by grants from a foundation set up by Ryan Seacrest, the host of *American Idol*.

But that's not the way we walked in. We were brought in through the crowded ambulance bay in the back, tucked down under the building in a concrete garage-type area. That seemed intimidating to me, and I made sure we were able to get Leah out to see the colors and fun of that place as soon as possible. "It's like an even better hotel than the last one!" I told her, and she smiled at that.

It was more than our surroundings that improved, though. As soon as we got settled and we got talking to the doctors about the treatment, it became clear that we weren't going to be locked in this facility for long. The entire treatment would last for two years. Two *years*. That was hard to swallow right there. But the good news was that the treatment would only require her to be in the hospital for five days at a time—assuming everything went well. She'd come in and get five days of treatment, then get twenty-one days off to rest and recover. Then she'd come in for five days again, and so forth, until they saw the results they wanted to see.

To me, that sounded doable. It sounded like something we could handle. I thought of it like a workout routine. Like a practice schedule. I could wrap my mind around it.

Then we got ready for Leah's first treatment. I had this vision in my head that "chemo" was going into some sort of special room with big machines or something, more like a CAT scan–type of experience. I had no idea that it happened in a bed or a chair, with nothing but an IV drip.

The MIBG was a radiation therapy geared especially for children with neuroblastoma, which was combined with chemotherapy in order to shrink the mass in her stomach. It was aggressive. It had to be. They warned us that in addition to losing her hair, she would also likely throw up a lot and feel really tired. I wasn't clear whether all that was going to happen the moment that drip started flowing into her little veins, so I was real nervous as we sat there waiting.

When a nurse arrived to start the chemo, it was just me and Leah in the room. I was shocked when all that nurse did was bring in a new little plastic bag to hang on the IV pole. "Is that really it?" I asked her.

I sat up on the bed with Leah as it started, and we did a little puzzle together, and she was all smiles and happy. I was just pretending to be happy, not knowing what was going to happen. I half expected her hair to start falling out right then and there.

I kept glancing up at that little bag, and the tube underneath it going drip, drip, drip, and thinking, *I can't believe she's really getting chemo right now.*

Leah didn't seem to be reacting negatively to the chemo at all. She showed no adverse signs on day one or on day two.

I went back to Asha's apartment for a couple of hours one of those nights, and she had a couple of friends over. Someone told a joke, and everyone started laughing, including me. But it didn't feel right. I stopped myself from laughing. What did I think was so funny when my daughter was in the hospital fighting for her life?

That night I started to think about something my coaches had told us: when you stop having fun, you've already lost the game. And I made a decision that I wasn't going to let cancer steal our joy.

I told Asha about it, and she prayed with me. She asked God to help me find peace and understanding, so I could be my best self for Leah. Then she prayed that I wouldn't stop laughing. She prayed that I wouldn't give up on life just because we were in this fight, and that Leah would be able to keep laughing too.

That really hit home. My girl *liked* to laugh. She was full of smiles and laughter for *everybody*. She smiled every time I walked in the room. I needed to not lose sight of the fact that she was still Leah, and I was still me, even though she was fighting this disease and I was right in that fight with her.

But then on day three, the side effects of the chemo kicked in. Leah started throwing up. She was miserable. She lay back in her bed looking all exhausted again, like she did on the day of her diagnosis. It took everything in me not to break down crying.

"It's going to be okay," I kept telling her. "I'm right here with you."

In my mind, though, I was scared. By the end of that third day I was thinking, *How are we going to get through two years of* this?

# CHAPTER THIRTEEN

# SPECIAL TEAMS

>> Time moves slowly in the hospital. Hours feel like days. Days feel like weeks.

It's easy to lose track of every other aspect of your life when you're behind those walls.

On Leah's fourth night of treatment, when it was just me and her in the room again, I dozed off on a chair. When I woke up in the darkness, I saw Asha standing over my daughter's bed. Her silhouette was backlit by the glow of the monitors.

She was praying.

Asha and I had only known each other a little over two years at that point. I could hardly believe the way she'd stood by me and stood strong through this roller coaster that neither of us ever saw coming. The fact that she was there, on her own, thinking I was sound asleep and still praying over my daughter—it hit me. Seeing that kind of dedication from the woman I loved, I knew right then and there I wanted to marry her.

I was convinced God had sent this woman into my life for a

reason. I believed she had already saved me from going down the wrong road. I believed now, with all my heart, that her guiding me to church is what allowed us to find Leah's cancer before it was too late.

After we got baptized, the pastor had come up to Asha and me one day in church and told me that I needed to make a decision: he said that if I wasn't going to take things serious with her and get married, then I needed to let her go. That moment kept playing in my head after that day, even though in my heart and mind I was already fully committed to her.

Now, I knew the time had come to show her my commitment was for real.

I had given so little of my attention to Asha since this all started. I was giving my all to my daughter. I had a feeling that was gonna continue, and I needed her to know how much I loved her and how committed I was to our future. I wanted her to know that I wasn't forgetting about her. Not at all. I appreciated her more than ever.

A lot of families that go through this type of crisis fall apart. And some of that, I believe, is just because it's stressful; but some of it comes from people demanding stuff from their spouses that they can't give them at the time. Asha? She wasn't even my spouse yet, but she didn't demand anything from me. She didn't expect me to give her all the love and attention I was giving her before Leah's diagnosis because she knew I was going through so much. I felt like, once again, she showed me that she wasn't a selfish person.

A selfish person who has no ties and can walk away whenever they want to couldn't go through something like this and stick around. Only an *un*selfish person could do that. Having already seen her level of commitment during a trying time like this, I could visualize the two of us staying strong and being strong together, for each other and our loved ones, forever.

Now I just had to figure out how—and when—to ask her to spend that forever with me. I wasn't sure how I was gonna make that happen around everything that was going on. But I knew I had to try.

• • •

Before Leah could leave the hospital, her mom and I had to learn how to administer the shots she'd need on a daily basis in order to keep up her treatment between hospital stays. The shots were necessary to boost her immune system. Without them it would be dangerous for her to go out in public, basically anywhere there might be germs.

I had to practice putting shots into little dolls until I felt comfortable giving Leah shots myself. The shots went in her legs, and the first time I tried for real, I had to hold Leah's legs down. She started crying and kicking. It was awful. I wanted to give up. It pained me, but I knew that pain was worth it. This is what my little girl needed in order to get better.

The second shot got easier. The third one was easier than that. I hoped that after a while, it would just become another part of the routine. But how awful was that? Giving our four-year-old daughter shots in her legs was going to be part of my routine now?

They told us we had to watch for fevers, because the chemo would cause her white blood cell count to go low. A fever meant there were bacteria trying to take hold in her body, and while going through treatment, her body wouldn't be able to fight it off. That meant any fever at all was dangerous. Catching a cold was dangerous and could even be deadly. "If she's feverish," they said, "bring her back to the hospital immediately."

I took that warning to heart and hoped her mom did too.

Just one day after Leah finished up her first five-day treatment and went home to her mom's to recuperate, I got news that I had to fly back to Cincinnati for a required team check up. So, I got packed and stopped by the next morning just to say "Bye."

When I gave my daughter a hug, she felt warm to me. I felt her forehead, and it felt like she had a fever. "Did you not notice that she has a fever?" I asked. Her mom shrugged her shoulders. "You better take her in," I said.

"Okay," she said.

I hoped I was being oversensitive and that fever wasn't anything big, but I had to go. I flew to Cincinnati and went through my check ups, and the doctors said I seemed to be in good shape and ready for the season.

That afternoon, though, I got a call from Leah's mom. I hadn't been oversensitive at all. Leah definitely had a fever. They were keeping her at the hospital because her white blood cell count was way low. Leah was asking for me, she said. My baby was asking for me, and I wasn't there.

I told my coach I needed to go right away and I drove to the airport as fast as I could. I ran to the ticket counter and caught the next flight back to Philly. I hit traffic from the airport and thought I was gonna lose my mind. When I finally reached the hospital, I rushed to Leah's side where my mom was waiting, holding Leah's hand.

"She's alright, Devon," she said. "The doctors said this happens. We just have to keep an eye on her."

I was so glad my mom was there. I was so thankful for her, but I was also angry that I wasn't there to begin with. I was angry that I had to fly back and forth like that. I was worried what my bosses might think. I was worried about my job.

I contacted the Bengals the next morning and told them my daughter was going to be in the hospital for a few days longer, and they told me not to worry about it. They said I didn't need to come back now, for real, until training camp started—around July 21.

That was extremely generous of them. Every other player was

there going through minicamps, and I wasn't. They didn't have to do that.

I breathed a huge sigh of relief knowing that I wouldn't have to rush back and forth like that again. But I also knew I was on shaky ground. What good was having a football player on your team if he wasn't there?

Once Leah was out of the hospital again, I flew up to Cincinnati for a couple of days just to check in with the team and start to get everything arranged for Leah's move. We decided to put it off until after I started training camp, just to get Leah's second round of treatment in at CHoP and to make sure things were going smoothly.

I found Leah's mom a real nice apartment. I paid the first and last months' rent and security deposit. I called and reserved her a U-Haul truck and got everything set so she could come out at the end of July. We set a date with the hospital to make the transfer and everything. It was all set.

That gave me a little time to breathe—and to start planning my engagement surprise for Asha.

I came up with a story to convince Asha to help me pick out a really nice ring without her knowing it was for her. Asha worked at Zales jewelers. She knew a lot about rings. So right after Leah finished up her first round of chemo, I told her a friend of mine was getting married, and he wanted her advice on picking out a ring for his fiancée. So, she went out shopping with me, and she found this one ring with a gorgeous diamond in the center surrounded by a circle of yellow diamonds. It was beautiful. "It's perfect!" I said, snapping pictures of it and pretending to text them to my friend. "She'll love it. Oh man, he's gonna be happy."

We had made some loose plans to celebrate our shared birthday on July 11, but those plans fell through after Leah was diagnosed. We hadn't even talked about it since then.

I decided that would be the day. I started Googling all sorts of romantic engagement ideas. I called a beautiful old hotel in downtown Philly and booked one of their ballrooms. I told her not to make plans for that night, that the two of us were going to go out to dinner to celebrate our birthdays, and she seemed real happy. It seemed that little thing meant so much to her in the middle of this crisis with my daughter, that I would think to take an hour or two just to reconnect with her.

I loved Asha so much.

I told my parents and her parents and a whole bunch of friends and family that I was throwing a surprise party for her and swore them to secrecy. I asked some friends to put together posters of every picture she and I had of each other. I especially loved the photos of us when she was there supporting me through my elbow injury and my blood clots—these moments when I knew that she was there for me.

I went back through our text history and found some of the love notes I sent her at different points in our relationship, too, going all the way back to the beginning. My family would hold blown-up posters of these as Asha walked into that beautiful room, which would be covered in candles and roses, to the sound of a string quartet playing a classical version of her favorite John Legend song.

There wasn't much time to plan in between Leah's treatments, but somehow all of those plans came together quickly and easily, as if they were meant to be.

During that same period, I talked to Leah some more about losing her hair.

She was real worried that she was gonna look "ugly."

"Girl, there is nothing that could make you *ugly*! You're beautiful with hair and you'll be just as beautiful bald," I said. "Look at me. Am I ugly?"

"No," she said. "I like your bald head."

"Tell you what," I said. "Why don't we cut your hair today, so we'll be bald and beautiful together."

She crinkled up her nose.

"C'mon, we'll be twins," I said. "Forget that chemo making you go bald. We'll go bald first and show that chemo who's boss."

"Daddy!" she shouted. She started laughing, and she started rubbing my head.

"If we're both bald together, then we'll grow our hair back together, too, alright?"

Leah thought about it real hard for a few seconds and then said, "Alllll-right. Let's do it."

Asha had all sorts of hair-cutting tools right there at her place, so I set up a chair in the kitchen, and we got to work. I knew I would get emotional, and I didn't want her to see the tears, so I stood behind Leah as I took the clippers in my hand. My eyes welled up as I made my first few swipes. But then she started singing: "Snip, snip, snip . . . cut, cut, cut . . ." and I echoed her, and I said, "Look at all that hair!"

She looked down at the little island of hair that was forming on the floor around her, and she said, "Whoa! I got a lot of hair!"

We basically just made a big game of it.

"Hold real still now." The last thing I wanted to do was to slip as I ran Asha's clippers over my little girl's scalp. I took long, slow, careful strokes. I just wanted to cry with every line I made over her head, but I held it in. I finished the job. I toweled her off, and we both went into the bathroom and looked in the mirror together. She looked up at me and then back in the mirror, and her eyes got all wide.

"Whoa," she said. "We look wayyyyyy different."

"Yeah we do," I said.

"Hold on! I know what I need," she said. She jumped off the counter and ran into the other room and came back with a pair of sunglasses.

"Where did you get those?" I said, lifting her up so she could look in the mirror again.

"My suitcase," she said.

"You carry sunglasses with you in your suitcase?"

"Yup."

"Wow, you really are a princess. Or maybe that's why they call you the selfie queen," I told her as I pulled out my phone and took pictures of the two of us in that mirror. We posted them on Instagram for the whole world to see.

I swear just being in it together like that made the whole thing easier. For both of us.

Then something crazy happened: my mom saw that we'd both cut our hair, and she cut her hair off too! I could not believe my mom would do that. My mom had gorgeous hair my whole life.

There's power in being part of a team. Leah had a whole team in her corner, and I think my mom and me cutting our hair off let her know that we were on her team no matter what.

Leah went in fearlessly for her second treatment on July 1.

I was so glad to have my parents there, and Asha there, all giving Leah support. But it really sunk in with me just how tough this was on the whole family. I thought we ought to use the platform I had with the NFL to help share the stories of what families fighting pediatric cancer go through. It seemed like there wasn't a lot of talk about this in the media, and I thought maybe we could give a voice to the voiceless.

Leah loved that idea, and when I talked to her mom, she thought it would be a good idea too. So, we decided to go public with our story. I wasn't all that well-known in the NFL, but I definitely had a lot of people who knew me in Delaware and even more who knew me because of my time at Penn State. I figured we'd get some good regional press.

As soon as we did a couple of interviews, though, the press blew up. We wound up sharing our story with USA Today and ESPN. It became national news!

It was stunning how putting some of this in the press and sharing our story on social media made things brighter. The staff at the hospital and some of the other families we met were thankful for it. And we couldn't believe how many people started reaching out to us from all over. People we knew. People who knew our family. Even perfect strangers. All kinds of people reached out through social media and email, and some even wrote letters and cards and sent them to Leah's attention at CHoP.

We decided to document every step of the process from that moment forward, to really show people what this journey was all about. Leah loved going on Instagram with me. We'd always done that together, so continuing it just made sense. And the feedback made her feel like a star. It made her feel like she had a whole stadium full of people out there chanting her name.

Suddenly the story of pediatric cancer was in the news. We were making a difference. It felt like our personal struggle was taking on a deeper purpose in the world. It felt like we were doing something good.

If we could show the world how to fight back against this disease and have fun while we did it, we could potentially lift all kinds of people, including other families who were going through cancer. We could lift people and give them hope.

All we had to do was keep doing what we were doing. Leah loved the attention, and I loved the fact that she wasn't thinking about all the negative stuff she was going through. Instead, she was giggling! She was playful in front of the camera.

She was Leah.

The fact that she was in the hospital getting treatment again mostly faded to the back of her mind as we spent our days doing puzzles and playing board games together. We got some competitive games of Jenga going too. That's the game with the rectangular blocks of wood that you stack into a big tall tower, and then the players try to pull pieces out of that tower, one by one, without knocking the tower over. Leah loved it. We set it up right on the hospital tray on her bed, and she even got the nurses involved. At one point it was me and Leah versus Asha and a nurse, and when I stepped out to get us some food, Leah kept pushing the table with her knee so she and I would win. Then we'd start all over again.

We made that hospital fun because we had to. I didn't see any other way to get through this.

I couldn't help but notice as I walked those halls and talked to some of the other families in that hospital that a lot of people walked around with their heads down, almost like they were defeated or something. It broke my heart. I kept thinking, *That's no way to win a game.* So I decided that I wasn't only going to bring Leah's spirits up. I made up my mind to try to bring everybody's spirits up.

Whenever I walked past a parent or patient in the hallway, I said "hi." I smiled. If we got into a conversation, I'd ask leading questions sometimes, like, "You feeling good today?" or make suggestive comments, like, "Beautiful day, isn't it?" Anything to bring a little light into that atmosphere, just to get people out of that sense of defeat. I needed to do something. The more time I spent in that building, the more I felt like it wasn't just the cancer that was taking the lives of these kids. It was the spirit they were allowing. I knew from football that once you have that spirit of defeat in you, you've already lost the battle. I knew people often spend a lot of time focusing on what they don't want to happen instead of putting their focus on what they do want to happen. Too often people tell themselves, "I don't want to fail," instead of, "I want to succeed." The difference in focus is powerful. And we needed all the power we could get.

I decided I wouldn't focus on not wanting Leah to die.

I decided instead to focus on making sure Leah *lived*.

I promised myself that at no point in time would I let my daughter lose her spirit.

Which meant I had some work ahead of me: it meant I'd have to fight to not lose mine.

# CHAPTER FOURTEEN

# INTERFERENCE

>> By the time Leah was released from the hospital after that second round of chemo, I only had three days to make sure all the engagement plans were in place.

I didn't dare tell Leah about the engagement party, 'cause I knew she'd never be able to hold onto that secret. She had come to love Asha like a second mom by then, and she got so excited thinking about us being a "real" family.

But when I went to pick her up that day, before I picked up Asha, Leah hadn't taken her shot. Her mom and I tried to get her to lie down so we could give it to her together, but she just wasn't having it. She was barely out of the hospital, and she was just tired of all the needles.

"Leah, without your shot, you can't go out in public today," I told her. "I was planning on taking you to a party!" I said.

Still, she refused.

The risk of taking her to downtown Philly into a room full of friends and family was just too big. So I told her she had to stay home.

"Why can't I go with you?" she cried.

She was so sad, it broke my heart. But I knew I had to make the right choice for her safety. And I couldn't wait anymore. I had to go. I knew this short-term sadness wouldn't last. Once she found out that I'd asked Asha to marry me and the three of us were going to be a family for real—that happiness would last forever.

When I went to pick up Asha, I was real nervous in the car. I had to pull over at a gas station at one point and get out to make a phone call to make sure everything was all set at the hotel, and Asha asked me why I was acting so weird.

Once I was back in the car, I guess I was real quiet or something, because she asked me about that too. She had no idea I was gonna ask to marry her that night, and I think I was scared that if I opened my mouth I might ruin the surprise.

When we got to the hotel, we walked upstairs. As I opened the door to the ballroom, she saw it. The room was lit up with rows of candles on the floor, leading her toward the string quartet that was playing her song, John Legend's "So High." Our family and friends were all lined up on the outside of the candles holding the pictures and the signs.

She started crying and shaking.

"What did you do?" she said.

I just smiled. I was still too excited and nervous to speak.

We made our way slowly past all those people we loved, past all those pictures and memories of the last two years of our lives together, and then I held her hands and talked about all the reasons she was the girl for me. I even talked about that final moment that sealed the deal for me, when I saw her silhouette in the darkness, praying over my daughter.

Then I got down on one knee. I pulled out the ring she had picked, and I asked Asha to marry me.

She said, "Yes."

Right in the middle of the most trying ordeal I could ever

imagine, Asha and I got engaged. And our team, the people we cared about the most, who had all gone on this roller coaster with us and felt the sadness and pain of it in their own separate ways, they all were able to gather together in one room that night to cheer us on.

• • •

A little over a week later, the time came. Leah was resting at her mom's house when I had to tell her. I didn't have a choice. I couldn't put it off any longer.

"I need to go to Cincinnati for the start of training camp," I said.

"Why, Daddy?" she asked me.

I had spent time with my daughter, lots of time, nearly every single day since her diagnosis. Explaining this to her was one of the hardest things I'd ever had to do.

"I've already missed almost two months of team activities. I have to go back to work and play football," I said.

"Can I go with you?" Leah asked. She looked up at me with those beautiful eyes filled with hope, and it crushed my heart.

"You need to stay here and stay strong, but only for like ten more days," I told her. "Remember, the doctors said you can't be on planes and in airports and places where there's lots of germs."

"What if I wear a mask and gloves?" she said.

"No," I laughed. She was so smart. "Plus, I'll be working all day. You'll have more fun here. Your mom and Mom-Mom—everyone will be here with you. And it's only ten days until your mom will be driving up to Cincinnati, and then we won't have to be apart anymore, okay?"

She was only four. She didn't understand that I needed to work in order to keep her insurance. She didn't want me to leave at all. But she seemed to hear something in my voice that let her know I had no choice.

"Okay, Daddy. I'll miss you," she said.

I got back to Cincinnati just one day before training camp started. I'd missed all of our team activities that summer, but the Bengals didn't give me any problems at all. I could hardly believe that my team was so understanding. How many jobs would allow an employee to miss so much time just to take care of their child? I recognized I was lucky. God had definitely put me on the right team. I started to feel more thankful than ever for the way the Draft unfolded—and the fact that I didn't wind up on some other team that was less forgiving or even further away from my daughter.

I owed the Bengals a lot, and I vowed to give them my absolute best. I prayed on the plane back to Cincinnati, "God, please give me the strength and the focus to give this team everything I have to give on the football field, so I can continue to give Leah everything I have to give back home."

I prayed hard, and then I played hard—right out of the gate. I'll be honest: it felt good to get out on the field and concentrate on something other than cancer. The focus it takes to play football at the NFL level is extreme. It's almost like meditation or something, the way you're forced to block out every other thought in the world. I was good at that. Or at least, I'd been good at that in the past.

Even on the field, where I knew that if I thought about anything else besides football I could wind up getting hurt, there were moments when I'd get lined up, ready for a play, and then I'd think of my daughter lying in that hospital bed and my focus would slip away.

After a few days, on more than one occasion, I was missing my daughter so much that I found myself reaching my fingers up under the mask of my helmet to wipe tears away just before the snap.

Somehow, though, I played through it all.

At one point I told my dad what was happening, and he called the team offices just to check on me. He was real worried. He spoke to my line coach, Jay Hayes, and Jay told him I was looking stronger than anybody else on that field. I guess I was holding it together okay, at least on the outside.

I kept telling myself that all I had to do was make it through the first week, because after that, Leah would be in Cincinnati. I'd be able to see her whenever I wanted.

And then one day before they were set to move, one day before I was ready to see my daughter after all those difficult days away from her, I got a call from my mom saying Leah's mom wasn't coming.

"What?" I said.

"She's not moving, Devon. She hasn't packed or anything. They came and got Leah earlier, and she just called to say that she's not going!"

My temper rose through the roof. I called Leah's mom, and she said, "I'm not moving. Leah's staying at CHoP, in Philadelphia, where it's closer to everybody. That's my final decision."

"Why are you doing this? Are you trying to keep me from being with my daughter?" I asked her.

"Come back here if you don't like it," she said.

I told her that I made a sacrifice to leave and go to Cincinnati so that Leah could get the best treatment and have it paid for, so she needed to make the sacrifice in moving so I could be with Leah. She just said "no," that she wasn't moving, and I needed to quit football if I wanted to be with Leah because *her* sacrifice would be going into debt for Leah.

I didn't understand the point of going into debt if we had a way to pay for it. It made no sense. None of it made sense.

When we got off the phone I kept texting her, but she'd made up her mind and wasn't budging.

It's like the whole world stopped. I had no choice but to change course on everything we'd planned and try to figure out how to make this work. What was I supposed to do, take her to court? Try to fight this? All that would do is delay Leah's treatment. I went to bed that night thinking the most awful thought in the world, like, are we really having some sort of custody battle over my daughter while she's fighting for her life? Are we really going to have to fight over *this*?

The next day in meetings, while watching film, the thought of Leah not coming to Cincinnati took over and tears started coming down my face. I walked out into the hallway and called her mom again, begging her not to do this.

I'd gone more than a week without seeing my daughter already, and now who knew when I'd get to see her. What if I couldn't fly back for her next treatment? This was crazy.

I was sitting in a chair in the corner wiping tears from my eyes, texting my mom and dad, texting Leah's mom some more, when all of a sudden the general manager of the Bengals walked by me. That man knew very well I was missing a team meeting and should have been behind those doors. This team made it clear from day one that they needed their players to be 100 percent focused on football. And here I was, out in the hallway while the rest of my teammates were focusing.

I hoped that wouldn't come back to hurt me.

I went back into the meeting a few minutes later, but my mind was still on Leah.

From everything I'd read, I knew CHoP was a great hospital. We liked the doctors we'd worked with, and they had all sorts of positive patient reviews, plus they used the same treatment protocol as the one used in Cincinnati. So, I tried to push all of my anger aside, and I prayed to God that this would somehow all work out. And after practice that day, I started to make all the new arrangements that needed to be made.

Thankfully I had backup.

Since I wouldn't be able to be with Leah every day now, my mother stepped up and volunteered to take my place. My mother was living in Maryland at that time, and it would be a long drive for her, but she offered to go spend time with Leah as much as possible.

She was willing to make that sacrifice, to take extensive time off work and stretch her own budget if she had to, in order to give Leah as much time as she could.

"That's just what you do," my mom said. "You carry the pain for others when you need to. Dedication. Commitment. Love. That's family."

In order to get Leah healthy, sacrifices had to be made. In life, you often have to lose something in order to gain something. It's a choice. Yes, I love the game. Yes, I was proud, I was ecstatic to be a part of the Cincinnati Bengals, playing in the NFL. But I loved my daughter more. I wanted to be with her every second. So having to be in Cincinnati in order to keep our insurance was a sacrifice to me. A big one. And I wasn't sure how I was gonna get through it.

I cried a lot after that. When we had downtime, when we were in team meetings where my mind could wander back to thoughts of my little girl, I lost it. I'd lay on my back in the locker room and cry it out when no one else was there. But I always tried to pull it together on the field. Always. I believed that was what mattered most.

I knew I wanted to always pull it together in front of Leah too. I had to put my game face on for my little girl. But it was hard.

. . .

The team let me fly back to Philly to be at my daughter's side for her third round of chemo, and I managed to not cry in front of her the whole time I was there.

Somehow, she did the same.

The goal of Leah's first four chemo treatments was to shrink the tumor in her stomach in preparation for surgery. The smaller that mass in her stomach got, they said, the higher the chance that her surgery would go smoothly and her surgeon would be able to remove all of that tumor.

Thinking about some surgeon cutting into my little girl was too much, though. After her third treatment, all of that positivity and laughter we shared when we were together in the hospital went out the window. As soon as I got on the plane to Cincinnati, I covered my face, put my headphones on, leaned into the wall of the plane, and cried the whole flight back. I knew that every day she made it through chemo, every day she overcame the hardship of that treatment, was just one day closer to the day they'd wheel her down the hall for that surgery. And I was scared.

Asha held my hand. After we got engaged, she gave up her job and agreed to fly back and forth to Cincinnati to stay close to me. I needed her. There was just no way I could get through those trips away from Leah alone. But on that flight, I couldn't even look over at her, or I'd just cry harder.

Leaving my daughter and getting on a plane opened the floodgate to all of the emotions I'd held back the whole time I was with her. It *all* came pouring out. I tried cranking up gospel music to help get me through it, but even the sweet sounds of Yolanda Adams's "This Too Shall Pass" and Kirk Franklin's "Blessing in the Storm" couldn't calm my fears.

My football schedule was full. The Bengals practiced every day and played preseason games on Saturdays. But my coaches were generous enough to let me skip a couple days each week, which meant I could fly out and spend two days with Leah. I would sprint off the field on those afternoons, change as fast as I could, jump in the car with Asha, and drive straight to the airport to get home to my girl. I never let her know when I was coming. I always wanted it to be a surprise. And she loved the surprise every time I showed up.

But it was hard.

The two of us would get on FaceTime every day, and every day I would see the changes in her. She started dropping weight. She looked skinnier and skinnier to me as the weeks went on. And while we'd managed to stave off the shock of her hair falling out, we'd forgotten about her eyebrows. One day when I wasn't there, her eyebrows all fell out. Her mom told me she'd been crying all day (even though she didn't cry at all on the phone with me), and when I saw her on FaceTime, she looked like a different person. Maybe I'd been blind to it—maybe I'd ignored it—but all of a sudden, she looked like a kid with cancer. And here I was so far away, where I couldn't wrap my arms around her.

As soon as I got off the phone with Leah that day, I lost it.

Back at our apartment, Asha prayed with me until I fell asleep: "Lord, keep us solid, keep us safe, keep us strong. Lord, keep us solid, keep us safe, keep us strong. . . ."

Because of Asha, the next morning, I woke up feeling thankful and started talking about picking a wedding date.

Asha meant everything to me. I didn't see why we should put off a wedding—until we got on FaceTime with Leah.

"I want to be your flower girl," she said.

"Flower girl!" I responded. "How do you even know what a flower girl is?"

"Who doesn't know what a flower girl is?" she tossed back.

Leah insisted, and we agreed that we'd hold off on our wedding until she was healthy and feeling good enough to walk down the aisle ahead of us. I liked that plan. It gave Leah a whole new reason to get well. A whole new incentive. A whole new goal to strive for as she fought to overcome the struggles that were ahead of her.

Goals are good, and having that beautiful goal would be good for Leah. I knew it.

My football schedule and Leah's treatment schedule didn't always line up. So knowing she had the goals and the mindset to keep fighting when I couldn't be there meant a lot.

When doctors brought Leah into the hospital to harvest some of her healthy stem cells—the cells that would be saved to be reintroduced to her body to build her immune system after chemo was over and this cancer was gone—I was working. I couldn't get home. Leah sent me a selfie from the hospital right before the procedure, and I was so proud of my little girl to see her standing strong and smiling.

I was able to be with her for her fourth round of chemo, the final chemo before she would go in for surgery, but by the time I got back to Cincinnati at the very end of August, the official start of the football season was upon us. We had our season opener against the Ravens coming up on September 7, and I was struggling to get properly pumped up along with my teammates. There's a feeling in the locker room that last week of practice. A feeling that follows you out to the field. A feeling that everything matters more, that everything's on the line, that it's time for every one of us to get into our zone and perform at the highest level possible.

On the field, I'm sure I did that just fine. But off the field, I was still struggling.

It turned out that my stepping out of team meetings hurt me after all.

On August 30, early in the morning, I got a phone call asking me to come into the office. Because of the timing, I knew it was a bad sign. I told Asha, "I think the team's gonna let me go." She was speechless. I rolled out of bed, slowly got dressed, and made a five-minute drive that felt like an hour.

My line coach asked me how Leah was doing, and then he cut to the chase. He informed me that I was getting cut from the team. The NFL requires all teams to solidify their fifty-three-man roster before the season starts, and after seeing what he'd seen, our head coach decided I just didn't have my head in the game.

I understood. On a logical level, a business level, I understood why they had to do it. The same way I could understand why Penn State felt the need to fire Joe Paterno. There are consequences for things, even when those things aren't necessarily your fault, or even if you're not directly involved. The Bengals had a job to do. Their job was to go out and play hard and try to deliver the city of Cincinnati a Super Bowl. My head was not 100 percent in the game. It just wasn't. I couldn't give 100 percent of myself to anything except my daughter. So I got it. I understood.

But it crushed me.

The team wasn't coldhearted about it. Not at all. Before I left, they sent me in to talk to our head coach, Marvin Lewis. He and I had developed a relationship because he was real concerned for my daughter, and even in that meeting he asked me how Leah was doing before saying anything else.

"Look, I know this hurts," he said. "I know this isn't what you wanted to hear. But I also want you to know that we did our best to try to trade you. We were in touch with the Eagles and the other teams in closer proximity to Philadelphia, so you could get closer to the hospital, but none of those teams were able to take you on at this time."

What that meant, he explained to me, was that over the course of the next twenty-four hours, during the waiver period, any other team in the NFL would be free to offer me a new contract. But my contract with the Bengals? A multi-year contract worth millions of dollars? That contract was now finished. I would have no choice but to go home and wait a day to see where the calls came from, and no matter what, there was a very good chance any offers I'd get would be to go work somewhere much farther away from Leah.

He also mentioned that if I cleared waivers, he would love to bump me down to the practice squad just to keep me employed. That was a generous thing to do, but in that moment, it sure didn't feel that way.

I'd gone to bed the night before as an NFL Draft pick with a multimillion-dollar contract, and I woke up to news that my best hope now was to either move farther away from my daughter or get bumped down to a practice squad.

"I'm sorry, Devon," he said.

I went home feeling maybe more depressed than I'd ever felt in my life. I told Asha what had happened, and she was crushed too.

The two of us lay down, and we both fell asleep. I'm not sure if it was some sort of clinical depression, but the two of us slept for the next twenty-four hours. We slept away an entire day. I don't think either of us wanted to wake up and face reality.

Before the waiver period was over, I got calls from the 49ers and the Vikings—in San Francisco and Minnesota, respectively—asking me not to join their roster, but to join their practice squads. I refused both offers. I decided I would rather be unemployed than move that far away from my daughter, especially to serve on a practice squad.

Asha prayed a whole lot. She asked me to pray with her, and I did. I closed my eyes, and I held her hands, and I listened as she asked God to show us some light and guidance, or to show us some sign that we were making the right decision by choosing to stay closer to Leah and not join either of those teams—in addition to asking for Leah's pain and sickness to be healed, of course, like we always did.

The fact that being released from the team might mean the end of my career and that I might be losing everything I'd worked so hard for all those years hit me hard. But after praying with Asha, the part of me that wasn't scared and numb actually felt a little relieved. I was happy that I'd get to spend more time with my daughter. But then I realized that being released from the team would mean I'd lose my insurance coverage—the very insurance coverage that was paying for Leah's treatment. And that scared me more than anything.

So I decided to take the Bengals' offer and join the team's practice squad.

I wouldn't be a part of the team's fifty-three-man roster. But as disappointed as I was, I tried to think of it like, *So what? At least I'll be able to see Leah.* I was taking a massive hit to my salary, but that didn't really matter either, did it? I wouldn't have to travel for away games, which would give me more time to spend with my daughter.

And my coach had told me, "There won't be any interruption to your insurance coverage. Her care will be covered. One-hundred percent."

It was a blessing.

When I called my coach to tell him I was staying, I started crying.

"Yeah," he said. "Look, you know we're all pulling for Leah. I know her surgery is coming up. Just give us what you can, stick it out on the practice squad, and take the time to do what you have to do for your little girl, okay? You'll come back from this. I know you will."

"Yes, sir," I said. "Thank you."

"Alright," he said. "See you out there."

I hung up and explained it all to Asha, and she put her arms around me, and we both collapsed on the bed again, trembling. Asha remembered a little phrase from the Bible and said it right out loud: "In God, whose word I praise—in God I trust and am not afraid" (Psalm 56:4).

I still had my insurance. That was a miracle.

That weekend, the press went nuts for the story of my firing and rehiring. People loved it. The fact that my team let me go and then rehired me so I could keep my insurance for my daughter sort of proved to people that the NFL had a heart. It showed that they cared about their players and their players' families. It was great for the league, and great for us too. It drew even more attention to Leah's story than we'd garnered from the national press interviews we'd done a little over a month earlier. That weekend, even publications like *People* magazine, which usually don't cover a lot of sports, were posting stories about us on their websites. *People* is about celebrities. I was a second-year player in the NFL with only a handful of preseason games to my name. Leah and I certainly weren't famous.

"What do you mean I'm not famous? I'm a *star*!" Leah said

to us over FaceTime, wearing a plastic gold princess crown on her little bald head. That girl could always make me laugh.

She wasn't kidding, though. My agent started fielding invites from the *Today Show* and the folks at *Good Morning America*. TMZ posted all about our story. We had no idea just how popular our story would become. Then again, we weren't exactly paying attention.

The Bengals won the season opener against the Ravens that Sunday. I traveled with the team just so I could see my mom and see Leah while the team prepared for the game. But it hurt like crazy not to be out there on that field. I was proud of our guys and how well they played, but it just felt wrong to not be a part of it.

When we got home, Asha and I went to bed still reeling from everything that had happened in the prior week, and frankly, worried that some other kind of bad news was just around the corner getting ready to jump us.

In the quiet of Monday morning, Asha rolled over to me and said, "I think I know what we need to do. Maybe God's trying to tell us to make a change again."

"What change? What more can I do?"

"It's not you, baby. It's us. It's the way we're living," she said.

"What do you mean?"

"I mean maybe we're not living the way God wants us to. Maybe we ought to think about living the way we're told to live in the Bible. Maybe we need to go all the way—or, the opposite of going all the way, as man and woman, you know?"

I gave her a blank stare. I truly didn't know what she was getting at.

"Maybe we ought to stop sleeping together," she said.

"Say what, now?" I responded.

Talk about snapping me out of my own head. I truly did not expect those words to come from Asha's mouth. Our sex life was the last thing on my mind.

"I mean it! A man and woman are supposed to abstain from sex before marriage, and we're not married. Maybe we ought to stop. Maybe we ought to wait," she said.

"Where is this coming from?"

"I prayed. I've been praying all night. And I just think maybe God's trying to tell us something. Maybe we ought to start living right, going to church more, even here in Cincinnati, saying our prayers, not just some days but every day. Living up to the sort of standards God wants us to live by."

It was just such a shock. I don't want to brag or anything, but Asha and I, we got along physically very well. And that's putting it mildly. We're just . . . *compatible*.

But there was something about the tone of her voice and the seriousness of her words that resonated somewhere deep in me. I looked in her eyes, and I saw she really meant what she was saying. Clearly, she had been thinking about this a lot. I started to feel what she was saying. Oddly enough, I think I had been feeling it all along but pushing it down somewhere because I didn't want to believe it. It's not like God was punishing us for living in sin. I don't believe that. I just think that God was trying to show us, again and again, that there's a better way to live.

So right then and there, I decided we ought to change.

"Alright," I said. "Let's do it. Let's make a vow right now. No more until we're married."

"You're really willing to do that?"

"Asha," I said, "I'm willing to try anything. I can't take it anymore. Something in my life has got to start going right, or I'm gonna lose my mind. And if that means making a change like this, and if you think this is the right thing to sacrifice, then I'm willing to make it."

We hugged and held each other in silence for the longest time, and I swear I felt a huge weight lift off of my shoulders. This woman was amazing. She was my support. My champion. I wanted nothing more than to listen to her and to follow her guidance in every way I could, and I felt that guidance deep down as we held each other tight. Even though we weren't kissing or getting undressed or anything, I swear I felt closer to her than ever that morning. And in some ways, I felt closer to God too.

Simply making that promise made me feel different, as a man.

We aren't perfect, of course. None of us are. In the months ahead, Asha and I would slip up and break that chastity promise more than once. Being attracted to the one person you truly love is a powerful force. But we tried. And I think that trying, giving it your all, making the effort to live right in God's eyes—that makes all the difference.

Hours after we made our new faith commitment, the Bengals made an announcement. They were putting my team jersey, number 75, up for sale—with all proceeds from that shirt going to support cancer research at Cincinnati Children's Hospital. That's the same hospital we were originally planning to take Leah to for treatment.

The press attention to our story that weekend was apparently more far-reaching than any of us (except for maybe Leah) realized, because they wound up selling more jerseys in that one day than they'd ever sold of any player's jersey in the history of the team. The jerseys sold for $100 each, and they sold a hundred of them on day one!

If those kinds of sales kept up, it could make a real difference for that hospital. I swear it felt like a little nod from God, telling Asha and me that we'd made a good decision.

Then the very next morning, God gave us a great big nod and a big ol' hug: I answered my phone and my defensive line coach asked me, "Are you ready to play football?" I said, "Yeah," and he said, "Well, come to my office then!"

I hurried up and got dressed and drove straight to his office.

"What's up?" I asked him.

"Hold on. I need to send you to Marvin's office," he said.

Next thing I knew I was back in Coach Marvin Lewis's office. He explained to me that another player on the team had unexpectedly dropped out of the lineup, so they wondered if I could give them the focus and commitment they needed to put me back on the roster.

"You want me back on the fifty-three-man roster?" I asked. I couldn't believe what I was hearing.

"Yes," he said. "Can you do it? We'll still give you the time you need to care for your daughter. We'd just much rather have you here than bring in an outsider this late in the game."

"Yes!" I said. "I'm all in. Commitment is what I'm all about right now. You have no idea."

"Okay then," he said. "You're in."

And just like that, after my career had been cut and left barely holding on by a thread, I was back on the fifty-three-man roster of the Cincinnati Bengals. I didn't know where they'd put me in the lineup. I didn't know if they'd even play me. But they *could*. I wasn't a practice-squad player. I was officially back on the team.

No one will ever convince me that the timing of that call was a coincidence.

I went home and told Asha, and we both wound up shaking our heads in pure amazement at what our commitment to living right had done.

Oh, and by the way, the national media picked up the story of the Bengals selling my jerseys that day, and they sold *ten times* as many shirts that Tuesday as they'd sold the day before. A thousand jerseys, at $100 a piece. All going to cancer research. All because of Leah. All because we'd shared our story. And very clearly thanks to God.

By the end of that week, the Bengals had sold $400,000 worth of jerseys.

The news just kept getting better. I played that Sunday. We beat the Atlanta Falcons. The team told me I could skip Monday meetings, and our team's off day during the season was Tuesdays, so I rushed back to Philadelphia right after the game, spent time with my daughter, rushed back to Cincinnati Tuesday night, practiced hard, then played the following Sunday. We beat the Tennessee Titans. I made five tackles across those two games.

We were *doing this*. With the support of people all over the country, and the support of our extended family cheering squad, we all felt lifted and pumped up and positive through the rest of September, as Leah rested up and got ready to go into surgery.

I found a quote from the Bible that seemed to fit our mood that month: "We know that all things work together for good for those who love God" (Romans 8:28 NET).

# CHAPTER FIFTEEN

# HAIL MARY

>> Leah's surgery was scheduled for September 25, right in the middle of our bye week. Even *that* felt like God nodding at us. As if the big man upstairs took a look at the NFL schedule when considering when Leah should get her surgery and timed everything just right, so we all could be together on that beautiful day—the day when she would finally get that mass, that tumor, and that *cancer* out of her body.

But the day before surgery, Leah got real scared.

"Are they gonna cut me with a real knife?" she asked me.

At first I didn't know how to respond. She didn't need to know the gory details, I thought. She was too young. Too innocent. So in a typical knee-jerk parent reaction, I said, "No, no. Not a real knife."

What was I doing? I didn't want to lie to my daughter. She deserved the truth. But I was too scared to tell her the truth.

Kids don't quiet that easy though. Especially curious kids like Leah. She kept asking questions, and honestly, I'd never seen her so scared.

I tried to distract her with a puzzle. I pulled up some funny YouTube videos, but the girl wasn't interested. She was terrified.

I needed help—and I was learning where to get it. I turned to God.

"God," I asked, "what do I do here?"

And God answered. It wasn't the voice of God like some people talk about. My grandma used to say she heard God talking to her, in a God-like voice, like you'd expect from some old movie or something. I didn't get that. Instead, I trusted God—and the words just came to me.

"Leah, you know, I've been through a lot of surgeries. And I'm fine," I said. "I play football, right?"

"Yeah," she said.

"If surgery hurt me, I wouldn't be able to play football, would I?"

"No. But are they really gonna cut me? With a knife?"

I pulled up my pant leg.

"You see this?" I said, pointing to the six-inch scar stretching from my ankle halfway up my shin. "That's from the surgery I got my sophomore year at Penn State. The doctors had to cut my leg open and put screws into it."

"Did it hurt?"

"I didn't feel a thing. They gave me medicine so I would sleep right through it. The same medicine they're gonna give you."

"It didn't hurt at all?"

"I'll be honest with you, it hurt a little bit the next day, and for a few days after that, but they gave me medicine to make most of the pain go away, and the pain was only temporary. The pain went away. I've been healed and fine ever since."

"Huh," she said.

I hiked my pant leg up even further. "And see this? This was from my freshman year in high school. I was only fourteen years old, so just ten years older than you are right now when I went in for my first surgery."

"And did that one hurt?"

"Nope. Same thing. They put me under anesthesia. That's the medicine that makes you sleep, so I didn't feel the surgery at all. And yeah, it hurt for a little while afterward. I had to wear a cast from my toes all the way to my hip!"

"Really?"

"Really," I responded.

"Will I have to wear a cast?"

"No, no. And your scar won't even be that big."

"I'm gonna have a scar?"

"Just like your dad," I said. "Scars are your warrior wounds. It shows that whatever tried to stop you didn't succeed. You should be proud that you're able to show your scars because it means you're a survivor."

"Huh," she said.

I showed her the "warrior wound" on my back, too, and talked some more about how a little pain is totally worth it, because pain goes away. It doesn't last. "And once that pain is gone, once the treatments are all over, you'll be free of cancer and stronger than ever for getting through it."

"So, it's not that scary?" Leah said.

"No, baby. It's a good thing. You've met all those nice doctors and nurses at CHoP. You know they all adore you and think you're the selfie queen."

"Yeah," she laughed.

"So they're gonna take care of you. And this surgery is going to get that cancer out of you."

"Well, that's good," she said. She was quiet for a bit. Then she looked up at me with a big smile. "I guess I won't be scared then. It's okay. I want the cancer out of me."

"I hope so!"

"God wants it too. He told me."

"He did, huh?"

"Yeah," Leah said.

"You talk to God?"

"Mm-hmm."

"And He talks to you?"

"Mm-hmm."

I didn't expect the conversation to take *that* turn.

"What does God sound like to you?"

"He sounds *good*!" she said.

"Yeah," I said, laughing at the joy in her voice. "I bet He does. What has God told you?"

"He tells me He believes in me and to believe in Him, and if I do He will help me. And no matter what I go through, He just says, 'Be strong!'"

"He said all that to you?" I asked her.

"Yeah. But God talks in all different ways."

I was floored. Not only was I taken aback that God was talking to my daughter, and that she'd clearly been talking to Him; but Leah helped me realize in that moment He'd been talking to me too. And I'd been listening. I'd been listening to God my whole life, even when I didn't realize it was Him.

He'd been talking to me through my gut. That I recognized a long time ago. But He'd also been talking to me through Asha. He'd been talking to me through the voices of my cheering squads, whether it was the crowd in high school when I first walked back into the gym, or the fans in some stadium, or the support of my parents in the waiting room at the hospital. He'd been talking to me through the public outpouring of support and love for my daughter and me ever since we went public. In high school He'd talked to me through the voice of the therapist who convinced me I was ready to take a leap from a set of stairs. He'd been talking to me when He told me not to stand in front of that party talking on a cell phone.

He was now talking to me through my own daughter.

What I realized during that conversation with Leah is that God doesn't always talk to us with words, either. God talks in all different ways, including through actions. God had been talking to me through my actions—or rather *His* actions, and *His* plans—which He'd laid out for me my whole life.

What instantly became clear to me when my daughter's fear of getting surgery went away is that everything—absolutely everything I'd ever done, everything I'd been through, everything I'd overcome in my life—had prepared me for this very day.

It felt like a revelation, and that revelation changed everything. As corny as this might sound, it honestly felt like the secret to life was suddenly made clear to me, and the secret is this: God has a plan. We can't always see that plan, but it's there. Whatever you're going through is just preparing you for something else. Something bigger. Something you probably can't even imagine. You just have to pay attention. Learn the lessons God's trying to teach you. Stay in the game. Don't give up. Fight for four quarters. Overtime if you have to. Keep going. And someday, *someday*, if you stick it out, all that stuff that didn't make sense is gonna make some sense. It's gonna pay off. It's gonna add up to something.

I knew, and I would continue to know from that moment forward, that whatever new struggles might come my way, whatever challenges or obstacles might appear in my life, they were just preparing me for a future that God has in store for me.

That revelation made me less afraid.

Knowing that everything we do in life is about learning, growing, gaining strength, preparing for a path we can't see but that God is laying out for us—just *knowing* that somehow makes the task of facing life's struggles that much easier. Faith in God doesn't make the struggles go away. The obstacles in life don't magically disappear because you pray. But the fear of those struggles? The terror of believing that each new obstacle is somehow gonna be the end of you? *That* goes away. *That* makes you stronger. And *that* is powerful.

As Leah fell asleep in my arms that night, I believed then and there to my very core that all I had done, all I had been through, all I had overcome in my life had prepared me so I could be there to help my daughter feel strong.

But I knew the only One who could really make her feel strong was God. And God was talking to her. So I held her close and I prayed deeper than I'd ever prayed before, with every cell in my body, for God to see her through this surgery.

• • •

As we got ready to drive to the hospital in the early morning, it was game time. And the only way I know to get ready for a game is to get hyped up. It didn't matter that this was surgery. Leah needed to get hyped. So I decided to give her a pep talk.

I felt inspired to take a little over-the-shoulder video of Leah, sitting behind me in the car in her car seat. Although she woke up feeling nervous, as soon as I turned that camera on, she put a big ol' smile on her face.

"I'm ready for today. Are you ready for today?" I asked her.

Leah smiled and nodded, "Mm-hmm."

"You ready to get this cancer up out you?" I asked.

"Mm-hmm," she smiled and nodded again.

"Let's do it," I said. "Fist bump!"

We both made a fist bump toward the camera, and I posted it for the whole world to see—not knowing the video would go viral. Not knowing that millions of people would see it. Not knowing that television news outlets all over this country would pick it up and broadcast it on their morning shows and midday and evening newscasts. Not knowing that people all over the country would see that little fist-bump moment of ours and say prayers for my beautiful daughter.

My phone went into my pocket as we got out of the car. I

wouldn't find out until hours later just how far and wide that video went and how far and wide the support for my daughter went.

As we walked toward the hospital lobby, I asked her, "You got your game face on?"

"My game face?"

"Yeah. You've seen us football players, how when we're getting ready for the snap, we get all mean and serious, like we're gonna attack those players in front of us. We put our game face on, like, 'Grrrrrr,'" I said, bending at the waist with my arms down, flexing my muscles and making a big ol' mean face.

Leah laughed at me.

"C'mon, girl. Show me your game face. Show me you're ready for this. Come on!"

Leah stopped and flexed her arms and squished up her face and went, "Grrrrrr!" It was just about the cutest thing I'd ever seen.

"Yes! Game face! Grrrrrr," I said, bending all the way down to her level.

"Grrrrr . . ." she scowled, gettin' right up in my face.

We laughed and stayed in that playful, pregame sort of mood right up until they put us in a room, where she changed into a johnny and waited to get wheeled into surgery.

"Leah, I need to get serious with you for one minute, okay?" I said, sitting her on the edge of the bed and squatting down so I could look directly into her eyes.

"Okay, Daddy," she said.

"I need you to promise me something," I said.

"What?"

"I need you to promise me that you're gonna keep fighting."

"Of course I'll keep fighting," she said. "I'm strong," she said, and she made her game face again, "Grrrr."

"No, no, no, you're not just *strong*. You're *Leah* strong. Like super strong," I said. "You're the strongest girl I ever met. Leah strong's even tougher than Daddy strong, right?"

"Yeah!" she said.

"So, you promise me, no matter what, no matter how tough things get, during the surgery, after the surgery, you're gonna keep fighting."

"I promise," she said.

"Say it, Leah: I'm gonna fight!"

"I'm gonna fight for four quarters!" she said.

"Yes!" I said. She was so cute. "I'm gonna be strong!" I prompted.

"I'm gonna be strong!" she said.

Then we did our special handshake to seal the deal, with the kisses and everything, and we pressed our foreheads together as I wrapped my arms around her and held my little girl with all my heart, silently praying to God to keep her safe.

By the time they came to wheel her into surgery, our whole family was gathered around her. Me, her mom, her grandparents, Asha, her uncle and aunt, her little cousins—the whole team. We filled up the hallway, following along and surrounding her as far as they would let us go.

"We love you, Leah!" everyone said. "Love you!" "Be strong, girl!" all speaking over each other.

As they pushed her through the double doors, I called to her: "Game face!"

"Grrrrr . . ." I heard her call back in her little voice as the doors swung closed.

We all got real quiet.

It was all in God's hands now.

● ● ●

Leah's surgery lasted nearly seven hours. Seven. Long. Hours.

When the surgeon came into the waiting area, our whole crew stood up all at once. He looked overwhelmed. I don't think he was prepared to give a speech to that big of an audience. An audience that was literally holding its breath.

"Hi everyone," he said. "We got it."

Everyone breathed a huge sigh of relief.

"The tumor's gone. Leah did great."

A few members of our squad cheered as the doctor came over and quietly told us, "I believe we got it all. I was able to clean some of the cancer out of her adrenal gland as well. That's really where this all started," he said.

"Can we see her?" I asked.

"Not all of you. Not yet. Just the parents, yes. It'll be a while before she wakes up . . ." he said, and he gave us some instructions, and I didn't really hear any of what he said. I just wanted to go back and see my daughter.

When they took us to her room she wasn't there yet. They were waiting to bring her in from the post-surgical area, and when they finally wheeled her in, I barely recognized her. Leah was all bloated up. She was still sleeping, and it was real hard to look at my daughter in that condition. She looked almost lifeless.

The doctors and nurses told us repeatedly that her body went through a lot of stress during that surgery, so it was imperative that she sit up and get up and move in the next couple of days. If she didn't move her body enough she could get bedsores or blood clots from having such a long procedure.

It wasn't until the next morning that she started opening her eyes and looking around. She was groggy and grumpy and didn't want to move at all.

For two days my Leah wouldn't speak to me and wouldn't take any food—but I didn't tell her it was okay. I didn't appease her.

I whispered in her ear: "You told me you was gonna keep fighting. You promised me. Remember?"

I said, "I'm telling you, this pain is temporary. I know you feel bad. But this pain is temporary. It goes away. Just like it went away for me. You've got to eat, Leah. You've got to move. You've got to fight. That's all. And the pain will go away."

For two days we offered her games and coloring books and puzzles, and she just looked away or closed her eyes. She was so distant. So unreachable.

Her bedside table, the one we'd played Jenga on, was pushed way down toward the end of her bed, and we left a coloring book with crayons on it just waiting for her. Waiting for her to come around.

"You promised you'd keep fighting, Leah," I repeated. "You promised."

I was exhausted. I decided to rest my head on the couch across from her and nearly fell asleep myself, until, in that almost dozed-off state, I heard Leah's little voice.

"Daddy," she said. "Can you pass me the crayons?"

I picked my head up and looked at that beautiful face, and I smiled. I started to get up, thinking, *Sure, I'll get them for you*. But when I went to go reach for them I stopped myself. I sat back down.

Leah looked at me with a confused face.

"I could get you those crayons," I said, "but I'm not going to. If you want to color, you're going to have to reach out and get those crayons yourself."

Then she *really* gave me a look. I could tell she was thinking, *This man doesn't know what I just went through!* But I looked right back at her with one of those dad-type looks that tells your kid you're not kidding.

That look was all it took. Leah pushed herself up a little bit and said a reluctant, "Okay." She started to reach for the crayons, and it was really hard. She could barely move her body. I could tell she was hurting.

"You got it," I said. "You can do it!"

She tried again and again, and I kept encouraging her. After maybe three minutes, she fell back on the bed, looking like she wanted to give up. As her dad I wanted to give up, too, to just be like, "You know what? Here, take these crayons." But I couldn't let myself do it. I felt bad about it. It wasn't comfortable. But I knew that if I gave her those crayons, she wouldn't know how strong she was.

So I told her, "I'm not passing you the crayons." I said, "You need to get them. This is your moment to find out how strong you are."

Leah sat up and she went for it again, and after two minutes of grabbing for the box she pushed herself forward and reached out one more inch, and she grabbed it. She fell back onto the bed with those crayons in her hand and a big, triumphant smile on her face.

"See, I told you you could do it!" I said.

To me, that was Leah's leap from the top of the stairs.

• • •

That victory was important. Keeping that smile on her face was important. Bringing her whole cheering squad into the room to lift her up was important. Showing her the overwhelming responses we were getting from tens of thousands of people on Instagram was important too. It felt like the whole world was cheering her on— and praying for her.

I swear it took all of that support to get her up and walking later that day, but she did it. And *that* was important. Bringing her down to the children's playroom as soon as we could so she could color and play games with some other kids around was important too. She needed me and her mom and Asha and her grandparents and all of us right there, cheering her on in our own unique ways in order to get her up and moving.

One thing I loved was watching Leah style Asha's hair. My little girl didn't have any hair of her own, but she sat up tall in that bed and worked on Asha's hair like she was a professional stylist. It was beautiful to watch those two bond as Leah began her recovery.

We were in the children's playroom when I noticed a little eight-year-old girl walk in, wheeling a metal pole with an IV drip going into her arm. She was by herself. There weren't any adults with her.

When she came over and looked at the puzzle we were working on, I asked her, "Are you here by yourself?"

"Mm-hmm," she said.

"Where are your parents at?"

"I live with my mom, and she had to go back to work," she said.

"So, you're really here all by yourself?" I asked her.

"Yeah," she said.

Her head was down. She was walking around with that all-too-familiar hospital look.

Leah looked up at her and smiled and said, "Do you want to help us with this puzzle?"

The girl's face lit up like it was Christmas morning. "Okay," she said, and she sat right down next to Leah. They laughed and played, and I could see that girl's spirit lifting up.

I looked at those two working together and my mind got turning.

When Leah started to feel tired and we went back to her room, I asked her, "How would you feel if none of us were here with you while you were going through this?"

"Sad," she said.

"Yeah," I said. "Me too. You know, with the platform we have now and everything, maybe we could do something to help other kids and their families. Maybe we could raise some money to help girls like that girl we just met. Like, maybe we could help her mom get more time off of work, or bring her grandmother in to be with her when her mom's not here—"

"Just like Mom-Mom does when *you're* not here," she said.

"Yeah. Just like that."

"I like that idea. Can we really help her, Daddy? Can we?"

I could hardly imagine how hard it must be for kids whose parents couldn't be there, and I knew firsthand how hard it was for parents who had to leave for work when their kids were stuck in the hospital.

I'd also recognized that what Leah was going through had touched a lot of people. I'd been thinking about the fact that this was bigger than just the two of us and our family. But I didn't know what we were supposed to do with all of that information—until God showed it to me clearly that day.

God had given us a platform, a nationwide audience, a way to reach out to people who could make a difference. We'd already proven that we could raise a lot of money with those jersey sales in Cincinnati. We raised $400,000 in a week! And I hadn't even heard any updates as to whether they'd sold more. I knew that kind of money can make a huge difference in families' lives.

So the idea was born right then and there: "I don't know, Leah. I think it's possible. What if we created a charity just to help families with kids who were battling cancer?" I asked her.

"Yeah," she said. "We should do that."

She looked up at me, and that was the only approval I needed to hear. I felt once again as if God was talking to me through my daughter.

I didn't know how to form a charity. I didn't know how it would get started. But I knew it was gonna happen. I knew that the two of us and our whole team were gonna make it happen, together. This was bigger than us. There was a purpose to all of this. Forming that charity would become a new goal for us. Something else to reach for. Yet another new dream for us to climb toward in the coming months.

I knew that having dreams and goals in place was what would keep us climbing. Visualizing the future, seeing the big goals ahead, living those goals now—it matters.

It matters, just like the power of words matters.

That week, Leah received a gift in the mail that was perfect. A gift that I wanted her to wear, proudly. A gift that pretty much summed up everything I'd been trying to teach her: a T-shirt emblazoned with the words, "Future Cancer Survivor."

# CHAPTER SIXTEEN

# FOURTH AND GOAL

>> To our family, it already felt like our whole lives had been consumed by fighting this disease. Yet we were only four months into it. Four months out of what doctors said would take a total of *two years*.

The only way the medical community knows how to beat pediatric cancer for good is to get it out and then keep on treating the body until there's no chance even a tiny remnant of that cancer gets left behind. That means after surgery, even after all of that, Leah had more chemo and radiation plus a stem cell transplant still ahead of her. And there could be more if all of that didn't go as planned.

I don't know how anyone could face this journey without faith, without prayer, and without family. How can anyone climb that big of a mountain all by themselves? Even with all I'd learned, all I now believed, there were days when the climb ahead still seemed overwhelming to me—and I had a team, and faith, and training!

As me and Asha started traveling back and forth to Cincinnati on our regular Sunday night through Tuesday night schedule again, Leah kept smiling, and dancing, and being herself whenever I was with her—be it on the phone or in person. The difference was now she seemed a lot more outspoken about her relationship with God. And I stood in amazement.

One Tuesday when we were getting ready to go to the airport, right before I left, Leah gathered everyone in the hospital room and told us to hold hands so she could say a prayer. My dad looked at me and raised his eyebrows, and I looked at Asha, and my mom, and we all just had this sort of amazed look on our faces as Leah closed her eyes and asked God to "keep my dad safe on the airplane, and make sure he doesn't get hurt at practice, and make sure the Bengals win on Sunday."

That last part made everyone laugh. But then she started saying serious prayers, asking God to help her beat her disease. I had to step out of the room so she wouldn't see me cry, and she came up to me after she finished her prayer and asked, "Did I do something wrong?"

"No, no, Leah. Nothing. What you did was right. I just needed to step into the hallway for a second," I said.

At four-and-a-half years old, Leah was already stronger and more spiritually connected in her life than I'd ever been in all my years of living.

The further we went on this journey, the more I found that I needed new inspiration all the time. And sometimes, when I least expected it, inspiration up and found me.

That October, while I was up in Cincinnati and away from Leah, I happened to hear the story of Lauren Hill, a freshman basketball player at Mount St. Joseph University. Lauren was battling terminal brain cancer. It was inoperable. Her doctors said she only had a few months to live. They told her she wouldn't make it past the end of the year, and yet she was still playing basketball. She loved the game so much she was still showing up for practice every day in the preseason, even while her health was declining. The NCAA saw so much inspiration in her spirit that they agreed to move her team's season opener two weeks earlier just so she could be sure to play. Her story went viral and there was so much public interest that they had to move the game to the ten-thousand-seat Cintas Center arena, where Lauren wound up raising a million dollars for The Cure Starts Now Foundation, which donated that money to brain cancer research in her name.

Lauren was nineteen years old, and she was an inspiration. I had to meet this girl!

I set up a time to go see her at one of her practices, and meeting her in person was even more inspiring than I imagined it would be. This blonde-haired girl was five foot eleven and a powerhouse on the court, but she carried this childlike innocence about her that reminded me of Leah in a way. She was full of smiles and light. It's like you could feel God working through her or something.

I gave her one of my signed jerseys and asked her to sign a jersey for me, and just knowing that I was gonna take that jersey home with me felt like I was carrying a part of her spirit with me. She didn't go on a bucket-list adventure or something when she got her diagnosis. Her desire was to help other people. Her desire was to raise awareness about her disease and raise money to help fight it. And she did all of that and still pushed herself to go to practice even when she wasn't feeling good—it all resonated with me in a way that I needed to hear.

My back was bothering me again. Even though it had been ten months, I was technically still recovering from my back surgery at the beginning of the year. All the flying on planes back and forth was taking a toll on my body. I was exhausted. There were days when I felt like giving up. But from that day forward, every time I thought I couldn't do it, I would think of Lauren and how she kept going, how she kept fighting, how she found the strength to keep doing what she loved no matter what. In truth, my personal struggles were small. They were nothing compared to Leah's, and they were nothing compared to Lauren's. I had no right to complain.

In that one brief meeting, Lauren gave me strength, and I immediately shared that strength with Leah. I called her up and told her all about Lauren. After that, Leah started asking about her all the time. It was amazing.

Sometimes people can connect without ever meeting. Sometimes we bond through circumstance, and sometimes it's something more. Leah considered Lauren a friend, even though they'd never met. In some spiritual way, those two were bonded, and I knew I had to find a way to get them together in person in the very near future.

That opportunity came in November.

Leah was feeling good. Doctors said she was able to travel. I mentioned this at practice one day, and the Bengals asked me if I might be able to bring her and my whole family up for our game against the Browns. "We'd like to do something special in tribute to Leah at halftime," they said.

"Oh man," I responded, "she would love that. Yes."

I had no idea what kind of a tribute they were going to put together, but as we put the plans in motion to get Leah up to Cincinnati, I invited Lauren Hill to come join my family in a luxury box at the stadium that day.

It was so beautiful to see Leah and Lauren meet—these two powerful girls who were inspiring people and putting smiles on other people's faces while they fought for their lives. They lit each other up, and everyone around them lit up too.

Leah said she felt like a star based on our Instagram following and the media attention she'd had, but on that day in Cincinnati, she learned what it meant to be a star in public. It was like she parted the seas when she walked into the room. Everyone stood back and looked at her and smiled, and people broke out into spontaneous cheers and applause. She dressed in a Bengals cheerleader outfit that day, and the entire Ben-Gals cheerleader squad got together and posed for a selfie with my little selfie queen.

Stadium staff members kept coming up to her and offering to get her whatever she wanted: popcorn, soda, candy, all she could eat. We were trying to keep her on a healthy diet, but if anyone ever deserved a cheat day it was Leah, and this day was that day.

The attention and affection for Lauren was similar. People were just in awe to see both of those powerful young women in the same place at the same time.

When halftime came, though, the attention of everyone in that stadium suddenly turned to my little girl. Leah came right down onto the field with me, where she could feel the energy of all of those people suddenly focused on her. More than sixty-five thousand people were all looking at my little girl's face on the big screen and listening to our story. I looked around, and people had tears in their eyes. It just proved what I already knew: this was way bigger than us. God was working through my little girl to do something special, something more than anyone could have imagined when this devastating diagnosis first knocked us down.

Then the announcer said something that blew our minds. He announced that because of the extraordinary support of NFL fans everywhere who bought my jersey, the Bengals were able to make a donation in Leah's name to Cincinnati Children's Hospital—in the amount of $1.25 million dollars.

That took my breath away.

My eyes welled up right there on the field. *One-and-a-quarter million dollars.* How is that even possible? How could simply opening up about our story, a story not unlike what thousands of families go through all over this country every year—how could that cause such an outpouring of love and generosity? This wasn't something we planned or something we marketed to people or something we controlled or expected to happen. This was God at work. This was God at work through my daughter.

Leah was overjoyed. Even a four-year-old understands that a million dollars is something gigantic. And for me, to think of my parents up in that luxury box listening to that announcement together kind of blew my mind. My parents were up there getting treated like high-roller celebrities or millionaires, not because they'd won the lottery, not because of chance and luck, but because of their love. It was their love and support, their finding ways to overcome the obstacles they had in their lives in order to support their children and their children's dreams that led to all of this. None of it would have been possible without them and what they did for me.

I was seeing the results of God's work every day, living the results of His work every day, and every day I felt a bigger obligation to share that revelation with the people around me and with the whole world. Just like I wanted to give back in thankfulness for all of my success, I wanted to give back to God in thankfulness for what He'd done, what He was in the process of doing for my daughter, and what He was in the process of doing *through* my daughter.

• • •

The Bengals missed our chance at a Super Bowl run that year when we lost to the Colts during the wild-card round on January 4. I was just as crushed as all of my teammates over that loss—until I realized what it meant. My season was over. We had an agreement in place for Leah to live with me full time in the off-season. That meant I was finally going to be able to see my daughter every day without all that traveling.

Knowing that Leah still had her stem-cell transplant in front of us, Asha and I got an apartment together real close to CHoP, and we got Leah's princess room all ready for her so she'd feel right at home the moment she walked in.

It felt like everything was going our way.

We were offered the chance to do a children's book, to help

other kids and families battling cancer to gain the sort of strength and hope that Leah had in her own journey, and Leah said, "Yes!" We worked with an artist, and Leah wrote that whole book herself. All I did was ask her questions and help guide her a little bit. We titled it *I Am Leah Strong*. We announced that book in January, and people started ordering it before it was even printed.

We started saying yes to more media appearances, too, making plans for Leah to take a big trip to New York City in February, where she would finally go on air with the *Today Show* and more. She was even asked to walk in a Kids Rock fashion show during New York Fashion Week. My daughter was gonna walk a runway! I was holding off on telling her about that one. I wanted it to be a big surprise.

Then we *all* got hit by a big surprise—only this wasn't a good surprise. This was the worst kind of surprise we could've received.

On January 11, Leah's scans showed the very opposite of what we'd all been praying for. Her post-surgery chemo didn't work. The radiation didn't do its job. There were still traces of cancer in her body, and that cancer had spread. It had spread everywhere. From her hip to her chest to her arms—even her skull.

When the doctor said those words, I couldn't help but think of Lauren Hill. It was only a couple of weeks after our joyful day at the stadium when Lauren took a serious turn for the worse. She had to stop playing basketball. She went into the hospital full time. The cancer in her brain was terminal. *Terminal.* That word just kept rattling around in my head.

How could my baby's cancer have spread to her skull? How could it spread anywhere after all she'd been though, after how tough she'd been? After all the praying we'd done? After God had spoken to her and *through* her? What did we do wrong?

We were suddenly facing a huge fight again, and I was terrified—but this time I also felt better prepared for it.

Once we got over the shock of it, we had some decisions to

make. The doctors explained that we could do one of two things. We could put Leah back on the same old chemo she'd been offered from the start, which often had good effect the second time around, they said. Or, we could put her into a new trial that had just been approved by the FDA; a new trial that was being offered at CHoP and showed great promise, but had no track record of success because it was brand new. That new trial was a study of different combinations of drugs, and if we chose that route, Leah's name would be put into a computer, and that computer would randomly choose which of the drug combinations she got. They were both believed to be effective in the fight against neuroblastoma, but the study was to determine which was most effective.

"So it's a gamble," I said.

"Not a gamble per se," I was told. "Either treatment could work, but yes, one will be determined to be better than the other. That's the point of the trial."

Imagining my daughter as part of some trial, some experiment, wasn't easy. I just wanted her to get the best treatment available, period! But this time, we didn't have the luxury to research and wait and think about what we wanted to do. We needed to make a decision and get her back into treatment as soon as possible, before that cancer settled into her brain or anywhere else. The clock was ticking.

In the end, I decided to follow what my gut was telling me: the old chemo wasn't working for her. Cancer's smart. It changes. It evolves, just like viruses and superbugs that find a way to survive and live on despite the antibiotics and other medications we throw in front of 'em. Leah needed the *new* treatment. The most cutting-edge treatment there was.

"Okay," I said. "Let's go with the trial."

I told the doctors. And then I told Leah.

Leah was mad. She was hurt. She didn't understand why that cancer was still there. She wanted it to just go away. She didn't want to go into the hospital again. She knew what it felt like on those second or third days of chemo, when the vomiting started and she felt wiped out, and she didn't want to go through that again.

"And I don't want to lose my hair again!" she cried.

We started the treatment, and it was intense. Her hair started falling out again. She got real sick. But she never complained about any of it. She took it in stride.

"Pain is only temporary," she kept saying.

I sat at her side every day she was in the hospital.

My mom came to live with us and stayed at the hospital all the time too. Knowing she was there allowed me to get away and catch a workout every morning, which I desperately needed if I was going to keep my job in the NFL.

The new treatment lasted two months, and Leah took every side effect—from mouth sores to losing her hair—as nothing but "temporary."

She was in such good spirits that we were still able to travel to New York for a few days, where my little girl got up and walked a runway in front of a room full of fashionable people and what looked like a whole wall of photographers, all shooting their flashes at once. She went on TV and lit up for the big cameras the same way she lit up for my phone back home. And she left that town feeling like a movie star.

On March 17, 2015, we took Leah into CHoP for a new set of scans and tests to determine if the new treatment was working. The results from those scans weren't instant. They would take a few days to come in, they said. Which meant we would have to walk out of that hospital not knowing what those scans might have found. It was an awful feeling. A feeling that's so common there's even a name for it in the cancer community: scanxiety.

We went in that day knowing that if this treatment didn't work, there was no telling what might happen next. The doctors could very well say we were out of options.

I couldn't allow that thought to stay with me.

I couldn't allow that thought to enter Leah's mind.

I'd never even spoken to her about the possibility of not beating this disease. I'd never spoken to her about what happens if cancer wins, because I didn't want her to ever think about that possibility and picture what it might look like.

All we could do was go home to our apartment, wait by the phone, and pray.

# CHAPTER SEVENTEEN

# TOUCHDOWN

>> As we were driving home from the hospital, Leah's oncologist called. The three of us were still in the car, just pulling up to our apartment.

"Mr. Still, I know I said it would be a few days before the results came in, but this call couldn't wait," she said.

I got real nervous. Why would she be calling so fast? Was something wrong?

"Not all the results are in, but the results of the initial scans are extraordinary," she said. "We're all pretty astonished over here, and we wanted to share the news with you."

"Hold on," I said as I parked the car. "Let me put you on speaker. Listen up, you two."

"Okay, so, you know we had high hopes for this trial, and Leah is one of the very first people to receive this treatment, but the results of the first scans: they're NED," she said.

I knew that term.

She and I spoke the next words together: "No Evidence of Disease."

"Praise God!" Asha said.

"Does this mean that I beat up cancer?" Leah asked.

We all laughed, including her doctor.

"Yes, Leah. You beat up cancer!" I said, and she squealed with delight.

"It's very good news," the doc said. "We're not seeing any active trace of the disease whatsoever."

"So . . . does this mean she's in remission?" I asked.

The doctor said she couldn't say for sure until the rest of the tests were back—the results of her MRI and her bone scans—but from the looks of it, "We're pretty sure that she is," she speculated.

At that point she asked me to take her off speaker. She asked me to please keep our expectations in check. It was a little late for that, but she reminded me that Leah's chances of survival didn't change after this. Even if she went into remission, a child isn't considered "cancer free" until five years from their remission date. I knew that. The stem cell transplant would come next, and that would have to go well for this treatment to hold. Then the radiation treatment, and then ongoing outpatient radiation and immunotherapy that would hopefully keep the cancer away while she rebuilt her immune system at home and did her best to avoid other people's germs. That would last *months*. "There is still a long road ahead," the doctor warned.

In our hearts and minds, we knew that Leah was already a cancer survivor. It was over. The time left in front of us would go by in a blip. I was sure of it. Pain is temporary. She'd been a cancer survivor since she decided to fight the cancer. I wasn't going to do anything to bring her down. I wasn't going to say anything to let her think there was any possibility other than winning.

On March 25, her oncologist called to confirm what we already knew. She told us that Leah had no signs of cancer in *any* of her tests. None of them.

"She's officially in remission," she announced.

That date would live with us as one of two dates when our lives forever changed: June 2, the day of diagnosis, was the worst day of our lives; and March 25, the day she went into remission, was the best.

• • •

On April 10, I woke to a text message from my older brother, Tony, letting me know he'd just read some sad news: Lauren Hill had passed away.

I lay in bed a good long while just thinking about that amazing girl and praying that she was at peace now. And then I thought about what to tell Leah.

I had never spoken to Leah about what happens when cancer wins. This would be the first time she would come face-to-face with the death of someone she knew from cancer. I was scared how she might take it. I was scared how it might affect her.

My fears were unfounded. When I broke the news to her, Leah said, "So the angels came and got her?"

"Yeah," I said. "They did."

"It's okay, Dad. Lauren's with God. He'll take care of her," she said.

Leah never failed to amaze me.

Still, I knew we had some big fights ahead.

I got a call shortly after Lauren's passing telling me that Leah's transplant would start on the day before her birthday that May. I knew it was going to be tough.

We tried to make her fifth birthday special for her in that hospital. We brought her a cake. Then, over the course of her first five days, she received high doses of chemo aimed at wiping out all of her bone marrow. This procedure was to ensure no cancer cells were left so that her transplanted stem cells would be free to grow new cancer-free cells. On May 12 they came in and gave her those stem cells through the port in her chest, and it made the whole room smell like creamed corn. She handled the first sixteen days really well, always making the best of it and smiling and dancing on the bed.

But on May 29, something turned.

Leah got really tired. She didn't look good. She didn't feel good.

The doctors ran a series of tests, and we found out she'd developed something called VOD—veno-occlusive disease—which can happen due to the high doses of chemotherapy they gave her leading up to the transplant. As a result, the small veins in her liver were obstructed, which caused all kinds of problems.

Leah got weak. She could barely move. She didn't want to eat. Drink. Anything.

For five straight days she did almost nothing but sleep.

Asha and I kept praying. We never let up. But seeing my daughter so weak and shut down like that, it was hard to stay positive. Negative thoughts and worry kept trying to creep into my mind.

"God, please let Leah's light keep shining," we prayed. "Please protect her and heal her!" We prayed and prayed until one day, seemingly out of the blue, Leah rolled over and looked at us. And smiled.

She came out of it.

The VOD went away.

One more challenge. One more milestone. She would have to stay in the hospital for weeks, just to be safe, but as long as she was smiling, I knew she would make it. She would make it. I kept telling myself, "*She'll make it.*"

That July, we got a call that ESPN wanted to honor the two of us with a special award at the ESPYs: the Jimmy V Award for Perseverance. Leah's immune system was far too weak for her to make a flight to Los Angeles and mingle with thousands of people at an awards show. So, we decided that I would accept the award in person, and she would send a taped message they could broadcast that night.

In front of that audience, I talked about the moment when Leah tried to scoop the cancer out of her stomach and put it into mine, and how that gave me hope that God was answering my prayers. I talked about the crushing moment when the doctors told me the cancer had spread, and how I felt like giving up, but I couldn't—because I'd preached to my daughter about never giving up, so how could I give up myself? And I spoke about how God ultimately did answer our prayers when Leah went into remission. To feel the wash of applause from that audience was healing for me. It really was.

Then I thanked the Bengals. "Y'all set the example for corporate America. Y'all let everybody know what it's like for an employer to stick behind an employee when we can do nothing for you," I said. And that got a big wave of applause too.

I tried to thank everyone I could think of in that speech—including Asha. I got all teary-eyed talking to her, addressing my words right to her, thanking her for being patient and putting up with the fact that our wedding was on hold because we wanted to wait until Leah was healthy enough to walk in with us. "You stood by my side. You let me know that you was gonna be there for me," I said. "I thank you for being so unselfish. And I promise you, I'm gonna try to give you the wedding of your dreams. That don't mean that when we leave here tonight, you go back and start dreaming of some crazy stuff and throwing the budget up—"

The audience laughed and applauded at that, just before I thanked my parents, and thanked Leah, who I knew was watching at home.

It felt like the whole world watched that speech. I got calls and texts from just about everybody I'd ever met. The speech went viral over the next couple of days, and I started fielding offers from corporations who wanted me to come speak to their companies. It was crazy. I couldn't take advantage of 90 percent of the offers that came in, though, because I had to get back to the life I already had.

Leah started her next treatment that July, right before it was time for me to get back to Cincinnati for Bengals training camp. If all went well, this outpatient proton radiation would be her last treatment. The hospital even had a special bell that they let kids ring when that part of their treatment was over—just to mark how special of an occasion it is that they've made it this far. Leah couldn't wait to ring that bell.

And she did ring that bell, eighteen days later, when she completed her radiation therapy.

My baby's last treatment in that hospital was finished.

# CHAPTER EIGHTEEN

# THE
# CHAMPIONSHIP

>> Asha and I decided there was no time like the present to start focusing on the future. Getting married, to us, was as much about the three of us becoming a family as it was Asha and me becoming man and wife. We knew that all of Leah's treatments would be behind us by the spring of 2016. And since Leah was so excited about becoming a flower girl and the three of us becoming a family, we decided we ought to get started planning.

I also had high hopes heading into that season with the Bengals. I put a lot of work into getting back into shape, and I was making the front of articles because the coaches kept telling the press that I was playing "like a man on a mission."

But on September 5, right before our season opener, I woke to an early morning phone call. They asked me to come into the office. I wound up in Marvin Lewis's office, where he told me that they'd decided to cut me from the team. They weren't bumping me down to the practice squad this time, either. This cut was for real.

Coach Lewis told me they wanted to "focus on football" that year. I knew exactly what he meant by that. Even though I was playing at my best, I had chosen to skip our off-season workouts that summer when Leah was diagnosed with VOD.

I knew that wasn't a good look, and I knew the risks when I made that decision. But I was more than willing to sacrifice my dreams so that one day Leah could live hers. I knew I could get football back one day if I lost it, but I couldn't get Leah back if I lost her.

Still, when the coach said those words, I was disappointed.

It hurt.

The Bengals had been more generous to my daughter and me than I would have expected any team to be, but I had also sacrificed a lot for *them*. I'd worked hard to get in shape for that season, and I was finally ready to give them my all. To not be given the chance to follow through on all of that was a difficult pill to swallow.

But there was some good news that came along with getting cut this time around. I had played a full season with the Bengals the prior year, which meant that my insurance with the NFL would be guaranteed for five years, whether or not I got picked up by another team. That meant Leah was safe. She could complete her treatments without any of us having to worry about the costs.

Plus, it was a good thing that I was home with Leah that fall after all.

It turned out that she still had one more treatment left: immunotherapy. That therapy wound up following a schedule not unlike her old chemotherapy schedule, and the repetitiveness of it all wore her down.

So, for one more season, I needed to be her rock. I needed to explain to her that the pain she was feeling now, which was more emotional pain than anything else, was just a different type of pain—and to remind her that pain is only temporary. Regardless of what kind of pain you have, it eventually goes away.

I also reminded her that another dream of ours was coming true: the Still Strong Foundation was up and running.

It's not easy to set up a foundation and to get all the pieces of the puzzle in place that it takes to start helping families the way we wanted to help them. But we did it. Our mission stemmed from one basic idea: deciding between keeping the lights on or keeping watch over your sick child is not a choice any parent should face. The goal would be to raise and distribute funds to help families with things like their rent, their utilities, their transportation expenses to and from the hospital. We would start with families with children at A. I. duPont, CHoP, and St. Christopher's Hospital (in Philadelphia) with a goal of expanding to families with children at hospitals all over the country.

Leah and I were both excited, and when we reached January 12, 2016, the day Leah wrapped up her immunotherapy and was officially done with all of her treatments, we were even more excited. We were ready to start putting all of our focus into our family's future of helping other families fight cancer.

It turns out I still had some troubles to sort out in my own family before we got there, though.

For as long as Leah had been battling cancer, I'd been thinking about what I was going through and how much stress Leah and I were under—but I was barely thinking about Asha and how *she* was feeling under all that same stress. She was just as involved in all of this as I was. The only difference was that I didn't have a choice. Leah was my daughter. I couldn't bail on her. But Asha? Asha had chosen to stick around. She'd chosen this life. And just because I had committed to marry her didn't mean that all of the stress hadn't caused some fractures in the foundation of our relationship.

Once Leah's treatments were over, those fractures started to appear. And they ran deeper than either of us had realized.

We needed help.

The two of us were supposed to be a team, but we realized we needed some skills, some training, and some new perspective. We needed a coach.

The two of us wound up finding ourselves a counselor who could help both of us learn to handle our stress differently than the way we'd been handling it in the past. We'd been under so much pressure for so long—from the treatment, from the various situations that came up in trying to create our blended family, from the ups and downs of my football career—that just walking in to attempt to talk to somebody about it felt like a huge relief.

In just a few sessions, I learned some new strategies to tackle stress differently and to handle my relationships differently. I learned that with Asha, and maybe other people in my life, I was sometimes listening to respond instead of actually listening to how she felt. If I wanted to change, I had to work on myself—just like in the game. It wouldn't happen overnight. It's hard to change old habits. But I knew if I was gonna be a married man, it had to happen.

The whole experience reinforced an important lesson I'd learned through this journey: when something's wrong, it is never shameful to stop and ask for help.

You cannot heal what you're not willing to face.

• • •

On March 25, 2016, we celebrated Leah's one-year remission anniversary with cake and lots of pink balloons.

And when she turned six years old that May 6, she partied like a six-year-old should with a full-on princess-themed party.

But most of Leah's attention that whole spring was spent thinking about and planning for her big day: our wedding.

We set the date for a Friday night in May in the beautiful, historic setting of the New York Public Library. That's the castle-like building on Fifth Avenue with the famous lion statues on the front steps—right where Carrie planned to hold her dream wedding to Mr. Big on *Sex and the City*.

The important part for me was just having my family there, and Asha's family there, and Leah there as our flower girl as we'd promised—along with a whole bunch of our friends who'd been with us through all of the ups and downs of the past two years. And thankfully, thanks to God, everyone we prayed would make it that night actually made it.

Truly, everything that night was perfect.

Asha walked down a grand staircase to a classical rendition of Alicia Keys' "Never Felt This Way," and I could not believe how stunning she looked. She'd picked out a sparkly, white mermaid-shaped gown that had her looking like a queen or a movie star out of some dream. She was more beautiful than I'd ever seen her. Leah burst into tears when she caught her first glimpse of Asha in that dress, and her tears didn't stop even as her smile beamed, making her long-awaited walk down the aisle tossing rose petals out in front of her in a sparkly pink dress of her own, custom-made to her princess tastes by designer Hayley Paige.

That's when I started crying. To me, this was so much more than a wedding. This was a celebration that meant we'd *made it*. As far as I was concerned, this was the end of the bad times and the start of a whole new life for Leah, Asha, and me. And in my vows, which I'd written for both Asha and for Leah, I said it right out loud, in front of all those people: "We made it through the storm."

Did I mention that my friend Charlie's mother served as the pastor for our ceremony? She gave us her blessing, and God's blessing, and sent us off with an order: "Divorce is not an option!"

That divorce line made everyone laugh, including us, but I also took it as truth.

Everyone tells you that marriage is hard work. And I knew marriage would be work. There was a chance marriage would be harder than I even realized, just like raising a child was far more difficult than I realized when I decided to have Leah at such a young age. But I also knew that a child wasn't something you walk away from when things get tough. And because of everything we'd been through, I knew that marriage wasn't something I'd ever walk away from just 'cause things got tough either. I realized that real love isn't about finding someone you never fight with; it's about finding someone you're willing to fight for.

I'd built a foundation of faith with Asha that I truly believed would sustain us for the long game. No matter what obstacles might lay ahead.

When Charlie's mom said, "You may now kiss the bride," I kissed Asha with all the love I had, all the love I'd ever felt for her all running through my body from my toes straight up to our lips.

"Ladies and gentlemen," she said. "I introduce to you . . . Mr. and Mrs. Devon Still!"

We walked down the aisle hand in hand with Leah trailing right behind us and everyone applauding and smiling and taking pictures. We felt like the king and queen of New York.

Leah took the microphone and gave the first toast of the evening. She looked so cute, standing there in the spotlight, looking out on that crowd of two hundred loving faces.

All those people in that room had sent so much love and so many prayers to that girl. I know they were all feeling proud and happy to see her standing there. She could have said anything, and it would have melted their hearts. But what she chose to say—I think it's clear that she recognized all the love in that room belonged to her as much as it did to Asha and me.

"Thank you for supporting me," she said.

Everybody said, "Awwww," and started applauding for her.

Then she said, "I love my new family," and everyone just about lost it.

She turned and ran over and gave me a great big hug, then gave Asha a big bear hug, and I swear there wasn't a dry eye in the house.

It was all she needed to say. It was perfect.

Then she stood up tall and raised the microphone to her mouth again and said, "Now let's party!"

The music came up, and we *all* started dancing. At one point, Leah and Asha and I got up and did a new-family dance we'd worked out together to "Uptown Funk." Yeah, that's right, those two got me up and dancing silly in public, in front of all those people. And it felt *good*.

If dancing with my daughter at our wedding was the only video the whole world ever saw of me, then that would be fine with me.

Sure, I was excited to build my football legacy. I was looking forward to getting back on the field the next season and finally playing my heart out for a new team, with my head fully engaged in the game. But I knew what was far more important was the legacy I was already building with this family. The legacy that my parents had put into motion. The legacy that Asha was helping me build by bringing faith into my life—the faith that was missing before I met her, even though God was clearly working with us, and for us, right from the start.

As the music played, I gathered Leah up into my arms on the dance floor and looked at her smiling face, and I pulled Asha onto that floor with us and wrapped my arms around the two of them. We started spinning and laughing in all that love, and I thanked God. I thanked God for everything. All of it. Everything that had brought us together and brought us to this beautiful day.

We were *here*. My parents were here. Our families were here. Our friends were here. Leah, my daughter, was *here*.

After everything we'd been through, everything we'd faced, our team was still in the game. And as far as I was concerned, we'd already won ourselves a championship.

# AFTERWORD

>> Just before we finished writing this book, Leah celebrated her third year of remission. She celebrated it with a big crowd of supporters at the Second Annual Still Strong Foundation Gala in Philadelphia—knowing that her story is still growing, still inspiring, still helping families who are facing the struggles she faced.

By the time the book comes out, we'll be closing in on her fourth year of remission—one year away from officially being able to say to the world, "I'm cancer free!"

She's doing great. Leah is her full-on, dancing, laughing, smiling self, and growing up so fast I can hardly believe it. She's going to school and living an everyday life not unlike most young girls live—which is pretty extraordinary when you stop and think about it.

As for me? I got picked up by the Houston Texans, and just when I was having my best game ever with that team, I got injured. I had to get surgery. My one-year deal with that team expired, and I got picked up by the New York Jets. But that didn't last either. I finally decided, "Devon, enough!"

At twenty-eight years old, I retired from the NFL. I retired from football. People thought I was crazy. I still showed all kinds of promise, they said.

But I knew I had a higher calling.

People tend to think the goal of life is to get to the top of the mountain. That's what I thought myself. By making it to the NFL, I accomplished that goal, and what I saw at the top of that hill wasn't what I expected. Once I was at the peak, I realized there were other mountains I wanted to climb. I realized the journey I'd taken to get to the top was more important than actually reaching it—because that journey I'd taken had prepared me for the climbs that lay ahead.

Since retiring from the NFL, I've fielded invitations from all over America asking me to come talk to people from all different walks of life. People want to understand how I developed the mindset to overcome life's toughest obstacles. They want a look at the winning playbook! They want to hear some of the stories I've shared with you right here in this book. But they also want to get a pep talk for their own lives and learn how to overcome their own struggles. Mostly, they want to get inspired about going after their dreams.

There are lots of examples I could share here, but there's one speech I gave while I was working on this book that really stands out to me. The principal of a big middle school in New Jersey invited me to come speak to his students, and when I walked into that building, I was blown away. They didn't just bring me in for a quick speech. They turned their entire school day into a "Leah Strong"-themed day full of learning about cancer and the fighting spirit my daughter represents. They printed up bright yellow "Leah Strong" T-shirts for everyone in the school to wear, staff and students alike. They put together workshops and had kids do an assembly line putting together care packages for pediatric cancer patients at two local hospitals.

Leah and me together, we *caused* that.

When it came time to gather all of those students and staff members in the gym for my speech, I wound up pouring my heart out for forty minutes straight, getting those kids *and* adults fired up about what they could accomplish in their own lives.

"Not everybody is willing to go the distance," I told them. "And you got to ask yourself, when things get tough, are you willing to put in the extra work?" I shared my philosophy on being what you want to be *right now*, whether it's a surgeon, a mechanic, or an NFL player. I walked them through my struggles, and Leah's struggles, and when they'd listened long enough, I got them interactive, shouting, "I'm beautiful! I'm strong enough! I'm smart enough!" as one big group.

When it was all over, it took two hours to pose for pictures with those kids and sign all the autographs they wanted me to sign.

Seeing a school put something like that together, feeling the energy of those hundreds of kids all gathered around our story and learning from it, there is no question in my mind: sharing His inspiration was the something bigger God had planned for me all along.

I'm not sure what life will hold for us all next, but I know there will be more challenges ahead. That's life. I still believe the struggle only makes me stronger, and somehow it's all a part of God's bigger plan.

Way back in my earliest memories of playing basketball with my dad, I remember he used to tell me, "You're not gonna get any better if I go easy on you now, are you?" Those were some pretty great words of wisdom, because after all we've been through, I think God is telling us the very same thing.

So, I just want to say to you, however you pray, please make sure that you keep praying. God will show you the right way. Keep listening for Him—through the people you love, the people who support you, and the experiences of your own life—and if you're not "living right" right now, don't get down on yourself. Work on it!

We all live wrong at some point in time, and then something happens that draws us to God. You don't generally see people with everything right in their lives suddenly turn to God. It's *broken* people who go to God seeking answers. I think that's when God wants you to come, so He can help put things back together for you.

He wants you at your weakest. That is definitely when He found me.

Only after He found me did he show me what He could do, through my daughter's journey—and my daughter's healing.

Don't be afraid to allow yourself to be found.

I hope you'll remember our story. Hopefully it will continue to remind you to keep looking forward and to know that God is always there—even when it's dark, when you can't see Him.

I know that whatever comes next for my family, no matter how tough it is, we'll keep growing. We'll keep experiencing God's greatness, and we'll keep sharing it with others too. Leah and Asha and I together want to do all we can to keep inspiring people with our story—because we know that's what He wants us to do.

As for your journey? If you're down in the game of life, please remember this: keep giving it everything you have. No matter what the scoreboard says, you have to fight for four quarters. Sometimes overtime if it calls for it. Because as long as there's time left on the clock, as long as you're still alive, you're still in the game.

It's game time. Let's work!

# ACKNOWLEDGMENTS

Dear God,

Growing up, I never knew just how perfect my imperfect life really was. Every person you placed in my life and every obstacle that was laid out in front of me was designed to help me become who I am today. As a child, I didn't have everything I wanted, but today, as a man of God, I know I had everything I needed: a loving mom and dad who, despite not having both of their parents fully present in their lives, did everything they could to make sure we felt the love and support they yearned for; a brother who motivated me and pushed me to be the best competitor I could be; and a sister who continues to raise the bar in our family. You blessed me with coaches like Coach Kerry, Coach Paterno, and Coach Johnson who taught me just as much about life as they did about football. You brought Asha into my life when you knew I would need a strong woman to lift me up when I fell down. She not only stuck by my side through the worst years of my life, but she led me back to you. I feel like I can never thank you enough for Leah, but that doesn't mean I won't try. Sometimes I catch myself staring at her and thanking you that she is still here. I lost a lot of things since she was diagnosed that I thought were important, like the title "NFL player," but the title I'm forever grateful I still have is "Dad." I'm thankful that you brought Mark and me together to create a book that we pray will touch the lives of people all over the globe. Thank you for my new family at HarperCollins Christian Publishing who believed in my story and gave me a chance to share it with the world. I don't know where this book will take me in this new phase of my life, but I know as long as I continue to do the work, your will shall be done. Thank you!

# TAKEAWAYS

It took a long time and a lot of struggle for me to recognize how God was working in my life. I hope that after reading this book, you've come to a better understanding of how He might be working in yours. To help with that process, here are some takeaways—a peek at my personal Playbook for Life—drawn from my journey and meant to help you focus as you tackle your own.

 WE ALL GET KNOCKED DOWN TO OUR KNEES AT SOME POINT IN LIFE, BUT THAT IS A PLACE YOU WILL FIND GOD WAITING TO HELP YOU STAND BACK UP. (171, 175)

 WHERE YOU ARE AT IN YOUR LIFE MAY NOT BE YOUR FAULT, BUT IT WILL BE YOUR FAULT IF YOU DECIDE TO STAY THERE. (35)

IF YOU GIVE UP, THE PAIN FROM REGRET WILL HURT MUCH MORE THAN THE PAIN YOU'RE IN RIGHT NOW. KEEP FIGHTING. (49)

➤➤ IT'S OKAY TO HAVE WEAK MOMENTS.
JUST DON'T LET THOSE MOMENTS
TURN INTO A MINDSET.

➤➤ SOMETIMES IN LIFE YOU HAVE TO BE WILLING
TO EXPERIENCE PAIN SO THAT THE PEOPLE
YOU LOVE DON'T HURT ANYMORE. (80)

➤➤ THE MOMENT YOU STOP HAVING FUN IS
THE MOMENT YOU LOSE. (185, 196)

➤➤ THERE WILL ALWAYS BE PEOPLE WHO DON'T
BELIEVE IN YOU—JUST DON'T LET IT BE YOU.

➤➤ IN ORDER TO CHANGE YOUR ENVIRONMENT,
YOU FIRST MUST CHANGE YOUR MINDSET.

➤➤ LEADERS AREN'T BORN ON THE FRONT
LINES, THEY JUST HAVE THE COURAGE
TO STEP OUT OF THE BACK OF THE LINE
AND WALK TO THE FRONT. (98)

➤➤ LEADERS HAVE TO BE WILLING TO TAKE
THE CREDIT, GOOD AND BAD. (113)

RECYCLE YOUR PAIN AND USE IT TO PUSH YOU TO GREATNESS.

 LET GO OF THE LAST PLAY. YOUR PAST DOESN'T DEFINE YOU, GOOD OR BAD.

 DON'T FOCUS ON WHEN IT'S GOING TO HAPPEN, JUST MAKE SURE YOU'RE PREPARED TO HANDLE IT WHEN IT DOES HAPPEN.

 ACCEPT FAILURE, BUT NEVER ACCEPT DEFEAT. (241)

 START BEING WHO YOU WANT TO BE TOMORROW, TODAY. (103)

 YOU CAN'T WIN FROM THE SIDELINES. YOU HAVE TO GET OFF THE BENCH AND GET IN THE GAME. (258)

 NEVER MAKE PERMANENT DECISIONS BASED ON TEMPORARY CIRCUMSTANCES. (138)

 PRAYER DOESN'T MAKE THINGS EASIER. IT MAKES THINGS POSSIBLE. (223, 234)

MAKE THE DECISION THAT NO MATTER
WHO OR WHAT GETS IN YOUR WAY,
YOU WILL NOT BE STOPPED. (151)

 TRUE CHAMPIONS NEVER GIVE UP
UNTIL THE CLOCK HITS ZERO. (226)

VALUES SHOULD DETERMINE YOUR
ACTIONS, NOT YOUR GOALS. (128)

JUST BECAUSE A PHASE IN YOUR LIFE
HAS COME TO AN END DOESN'T MEAN
YOUR LIFE HAS ENDED. (259)

YOU CAN NEVER LOSE WITH THE WINNINGEST
COACH OF ALL TIME ON YOUR TEAM: GOD.

SOMETIMES IN LIFE YOU HAVE TO
BE WILLING TO LOSE SOMETHING IN
ORDER TO GAIN SOMETHING. (252)

CELEBRATING THE SMALL VICTORIES
IS JUST AS IMPORTANT AS
CELEBRATING THE BIG ONES. (230)

DON'T CONFUSE DELAYS IN YOUR LIFE WITH DENIALS. GOD IS TRYING TO DEVELOP YOU SO YOU CAN HANDLE THE SIZE OF YOUR BLESSING ONCE YOU RECEIVE IT. (223)

 THE DECISIONS YOU MAKE DON'T JUST IMPACT YOU. THEY AFFECT EVERYONE AROUND YOU. (89)

 BE PROUD OF YOUR SCARS. THEY'RE SIGNS THAT YOU SURVIVED WHATEVER TRIED TO BREAK YOU. (220)

 DON'T LET LIFE HAPPEN TO YOU, MAKE LIFE HAPPEN FOR YOU. PUT ON YOUR GAME FACE! (225)

 WHEN THINGS AREN'T WORKING IN YOUR LIFE, YOU CAN'T BE AFRAID TO CALL AN AUDIBLE. (241)

 GUIDANCE SHOULDN'T BE TREATED AS A LAST RESORT, RATHER A FIRST RESOURCE. (254)

 YOU CAN'T HEAL WHAT YOU'RE NOT WILLING TO REVEAL. (254)

LOVE ISN'T ABOUT FINDING SOMEONE YOU
NEVER FIGHT WITH; IT'S ABOUT FINDING
SOMEONE YOU'RE WILLING TO FIGHT FOR. (256)

 THE PROCESS OF REACHING YOUR DREAM IS
MUCH MORE IMPORTANT THAN ACTUALLY
ACHIEVING IT. (260)

# ABOUT THE AUTHORS

**DEVON STILL** is a professional athlete, life coach, motivational speaker, and childhood cancer advocate. Now known as "The Comeback Coach," Devon launched his company, Still in the Game, to teach people all over the globe his winning playbook on how to come back from life's biggest challenges.

**MARK DAGOSTINO** is a multiple *New York Times* bestselling coauthor whose career has been built through the sharing of uplifting and inspirational life stories. His books include titles with Chip and Joanna Gaines, Daniel "Rudy" Ruettiger, Hulk Hogan, Eric O'Grey, Richard Rawlings, and more. Before becoming an author, Mark served ten years on staff in New York and Los Angeles as a correspondent, columnist, and senior writer for *People* magazine.